IN
THEIR
OWN
GOOD
TIME

IN THEIR OWN GOOD TIME

Michael T. Kaufman

Saturday Review Press

NEW YORK

Published simultaneously in Canada by
Doubleday Canada Ltd., Toronto.

Library of Congress Catalog Card Number: 72–88659

ISBN 0–8415–0229–3

Saturday Review Press
380 Madison Avenue
New York, New York 10017

PRINTED IN THE UNITED STATES OF AMERICA

Design by Tere LoPrete

For Pepa and Adam

Contents

IN
THEIR
OWN
GOOD
TIME

Introduction

When I was nine years old, a kid in my class whose name I can't remember, but whom I think of as pudgy with a waddling step, came to school one day and told everybody that his mother was organizing a Cub Scout pack. I thought it would be great to be a Cub Scout, and I took some papers home for my parents to sign. Then, I remember, I had my father take me to a store where they sold official Cub Scout things. I don't recall exactly how I did it—whether I just screamed or whined or whether I used gentler tactics—but I have the very distinct impression that I coerced my father, making him buy me a neckerchief, a wallet, pants, shirt, canteen, knapsack, and knife, all with official Cub insignia. My father did not have much money, and I think back on those purchases with shame. We were an immigrant family arrived in New York five years earlier in retreat from the Hun. We were Jewish; we lived, however, in an Irish neighborhood that was soon to become Puerto Rican. In school all the kids in my classes were Jewish, but they went to Hebrew School and summer camps and lived in another part of the school district. I think that my father, who is a wise and compassionate man, must have felt some guilt about my being different, or rather feeling different, from my classmates. I think that I must have traded on these feelings to get him to shell out for all those blue and yellow official things. All this is, of course, retrospective introspection. At the time I wasn't guilt-torn.

I remember I read through the Cub manual a couple of times and, dressed in my new outfit, went to my first meeting of the den where, with fingers raised in a scary solemn pledge, I vowed obeisance to scouting and was duly initiated. Later that day, after lemonade and chocolate chip cookies, we played some games, and one of the Cubs must have been a bit noisy. The leader of the group was a heavy adolescent Boy Scout. I guess he was sixteen. He singled out the boisterous Cub and as punishment sat on him. The rest of us laughed while this very fat Scout sat on the Cub for two or three minutes. The next meeting the fat Scout sat on some other kids. The meeting after that he sat on me. It didn't hurt, and I suppose I laughed while he did it. But I never went back to the Cub Scouts. I took all my official things and put them in the bottom of a closet.

That initiation into scouting, attempted and aborted in the fall of 1947, was the last time I joined anything until thirteen years later, when I signed a dues check-off card for the Newspaper Guild of America. This is not to say that I didn't want to join groups in the years after my cubbing days. I did, often and very much. I spent a major part of my high school years lying flat on my back on my bed, listening to a disc jockey named Lacey and bouncing a pink rubber ball off the ceiling and fantasizing. In my daydreams I was constantly surrounded by admiring and loving people whose well-being was somehow entrusted to my command. I saw myself dressed in a shiny satin jacket with a name like Saracens or Marauders on the back and above my chest a curlicued stitched-out *chief*. Other times I was a Maquis leader, coordinating a resistance effort, risking my life for my comrades and feeling the exhilaration of communion with death. Later, after Marlon Brando or *The Battle of Algiers*, I would become Zapata or Ali le Point.

But those were daydreams, and in real life I refused to join any formal organization. In my first year of college I was asked to pledge a fraternity, and for a few days this invitation was fodder for my imagination. At the time I thought my reason for not becoming a brother was a question of money—membership would cost too much. But now I don't think that was it. It seems to me, instead, that I am just incapable of belonging to a group and that this inability is deeply rooted in my consciousnesss. Parenthetically, I am the only uncircumcised Jew I know, and I take that fact as a sort of primary metaphor.

Sometimes when I think about this sense of non-belonging, I tend to defend it. I view it in terms of refusing to cede autonomy to a group, of maintaining my freedom to think and feel anything. I recognize, though, that the price of this freedom of thought is a sense of impotence. That is, while I can believe anything, I can implement almost nothing, since by the rules of my game I am alone. I am not always totally blissful about my alienation and impotence. I think avoidance of responsibility and cowardice are some of the things that shape my outlook, and those are things I can't defend.

I ought also to say that I haven't carried out my views to the ultimate since I participate in a functioning family and since I work for a major metropolitan newspaper. The staff of the paper is certainly a group. Membership in it does require a certain amount of relinquishing of autonomy, but a lot less than do most other places. What saves it for me is that most people in the news business feel to some extent as I do. I know some reporters who will not even register by political party, thinking that such an act would circumscribe their freedom. Since the commodity they deal with—news—is defined by flux and change, reporters and editors usually tend not to be dogmatic. The rites of membership in this group involve the pursuit of an elusive objectivity. Privately we all know it's somewhere beyond our grasp, but publicly we go out seeking it, trying to come as close to it as we can. We are, I think, a society of voyeurs who feel compelled to watch things and tell people what we have seen. Some of us feel that if we tell it accurately, the world will be better; but most, I think, feel that watching and telling is interesting and fun whether or not it is socially redeeming. For an uncircumcised Jew, a reporter is a very good thing to be.

And that leads to what this book is about. It is about groups of people who like being together, who do whatever they do together not to make money but because they like it and would rather do it than other things. Some groups, like the Hell's Angels or the Young Lords, are very formal with strict hierarchies and set rites; others, like pool room hustlers and sideshow people from the circus, have more fluid kinds of associations. Most of the groups have at least several dozen members but one had only two, a partnership of old men devoted to a grand illusion that brought meaning and humor to their lives. One of the very nice things about being a reporter is that it gives you a passport to different places. I don't fully understand why, but I can telephone people and say, "Hi, I'm Mike Kaufman, a reporter for *The New York Times*, and I'd like to come watch you live," and people always say, "Fine, come on over." I can't remember anyone ever telling me to get lost, which often seems to me the appropriate response.

So this book is an outgrowth of the openness of the people in it. In each case I came to them as an outsider, someone who would stay awhile and leave. Everyone was very cooperative. Some people may have tried to make themselves better than they were because I was there, but that is a hard thing to do for more than a couple of hours, so even those who tried gave it up. Most people simply took me at face value: just a peeping tom who wants to get his rocks off, an assessment that is accurate enough. I want to thank them all for their tolerance. Anyway, I watched, and now I'm telling.

The Emperor of Byzantium and
the Creative Director of the
Grand Illusion

On April 11, 1968, the police were called to a rooming house on Forty-eighth Street where a man was lying unconscious. They found him in his fifth floor cubby, shriveled and tiny and obviously dying, at the age of eighty-two. He lay upon a narrow bed, the fronds of his imperial mustache carefully twirled and waxed. On each of his fingers was a large baubled ring, and around his neck hung a lead medallion on a gilded plastic chain. In the corner stood a silver-topped ebony cane, and on a small table lay a homburg. The man was taken by stretcher and ambulance to Saint Vincent's Hospital, where he died later that day. For the next three days the cadaver lay unclaimed at the morgue; then it was sent to New York University Dental School, where students poked about its mandibles. And so ended the life and reign of Prince Robert de Rohan Courtenay, heir to the throne and lost riches of Byzantium, artist, poet, lover, and jewel thief. *Sic transit gloria mundi.*

On an autumn night forty-one years earlier, the same little man swept into the Sir Hubert Cafeteria, an all-night beanery on Sheridan Square, leading the way through the maze of tables for a younger and somewhat bemused acquaintance. "Good morning, Prince," shouted a jolly, fat, and heavily rouged whore. The dainty man nodded to her and raised a finely shaped, thin-fingered little hand to shoulder height, like the pope blessing the faithful. Some cardplayers looked up and smiled their greeting. A few pimps, some actors, and the hashslingers behind the counter shouted welcomes as the prince led his friend to a corner table.

Then from across the room came the poet Maxwell Bodenheim, approaching to within a few feet of the table, where he stopped, glowered at the new arrival, and shouted, "Why the hell don't you stop all this bullshit!" A charged quiet fell, and then the man who was called the prince smiled a gentle smile and said, "Why, Maxie, nobody compels you to believe it. It is a matter of your generosity whether you believe it or not." Bodenheim retreated, the tension disappeared, and the prince returned to conversation with the young friend he had met earlier that evening at a speakeasy. Some of the other customers moved their chairs closer to listen to the story, which most of them had heard before.

"You asked me who I was, and I told you I was a prince and, though you are too polite to say so, in your eyes I read disbelief," the man told his friend, whose name was Harry Rosti and who shortly thereafter became known as Lord Rosti to his circle. "Now I will tell you how I came by my title. Actually, I am more than just an ordinary prince. I am His Serene Highness, Prince Robert de Rohan Courtenay, grand duke of the Byzantines, a direct descendant in an illustrious and unbroken lineage primogenitary, of their imperial majesties of the Byzantine Eastern Roman Empire."

The prince looked across at the smiling Rosti and commented, "I am aware of the questions in your mind. How can this be? How can a man sitting in a slimy all-night ham-and-egg joint be heir to an empire that was sacked and gutted seven hundred years ago? I will tell you." At this point some of the eavesdroppers moved away, for they had heard this part before. Paying no heed to his dwindling audience, the prince went on, "I was born in the Oklahoma Territories in 1886, near the town of Guthrie on the banks of the Cimarron River. I was born in a stable. But it was not any old stable, but a clean stable, all sparkling and bright. Not a stable with pigs and chickens and horseshit, but a spotlessly clean stable, all sparkling and polished with tissue paper. When I arrived, a Mexican priest who had foretold my appearance came to my mother and said, 'You see, Lady, you have given birth to a great man. This little princeling here, when a long-tailed cock will crow, he will be proclaimed emperor.' "

"But, Prince," said the amused Rosti when the account of the prophecy had ended in a dramatic whisper, "there is no Byzantine Empire anymore."

"I know," replied the prince with soft-spoken dignity, "and that is my mission, to re-create it, and then be crowned."

Rosti thought that was a fine answer. It was, he thought, a fine night, and there was something about this prince that really appealed to him. Here was a man, he thought, who like himself understood America, who understood life in a city where the spirit and the imagination were subordinated daily to mundane, pragmatic, and humiliating pressures. Of course, at one point in the evening he had thought the prince was crazy, but now he thought not.

There was a gentleness and a studied slyness about him that was very appealing. Rosti thought he would like to see more of the prince.

Rosti had been in the United States for only four years, but he was a quick student. He had arrived with degrees in philosophy and naval engineering from the University of Rome. For a year he had waited on tables in Paris and then he had come to New York, where he was welcomed by the only friend he had here, an old school acquaintance.

Rosti had come off his ship a tall, good-looking man, with a proud and massive nose and a royal bearing. His friend welcomed him warmly, and then the conversation got down to basics.

"What kind of country is this?" Rosti asked.

"Oh," he was told, "it is a very wonderful country, with many opportunities."

"And in what direction do these opportunities lie?"

"Well, in every direction. Here everyone has the freedom to work."

"Freedom to work? My God. Even slaves had that. What kind of opportunities are there for my spirit?"

The friend said that he didn't know, but that the economy was flourishing and anyone could make money, although the best way to make lots of it was in business.

"What kind of business?" Rosti demanded.

"Any kind of business. Anything that people are willing to buy and you are willing to sell."

"And this is ethical?"

"Sure it's ethical."

"How can it be ethical if you buy for five dollars and sell for twenty?" Rosti objected.

"It's ethical because you are rendering a service and getting paid for it," his acclimated friend explained.

"What service? A man needs a pair of shoes. You bought them for five. If he needs them badly you charge him twenty. This is honest?"

"Sure it's honest, that's business."

"Well, I don't think it's honest. You sell a pair of shoes for twenty dollars but you know they are really worth five. You should tell the man. The shoes are worth five dollars and then there's a fee for my service, which is worth whatever. If you think your service is worth ten dollars, you tell the man. The shoes are five, my service is ten. You owe me fifteen. That's honest."

"No," said his adviser, "if you say that, you won't sell any shoes."

Despite his demurrers, Lord Rosti paid attention. Today he lives in a luxuriously appointed apartment high above East Seventy-ninth Street. He realized soon after his arrival here that idealism was fine but there was reality that had to be dealt with. "I was here and I had no place to go, and if I had something that got in the way, which in this case was honesty, I had to set it aside, to put it in the closet. Just temporarily, of course."

With his honesty in storage, the young Roman of royal birth prospered quickly. His first venture was the development of a perpetual-motion scheme geared to the tides. A proper-looking Canadian fronted as president and chairman for the corporation, and Rosti sold shares on commission to the Italian community. By the time the Canadian fled the country and the offices were vacated and the scheme went poof, a period of six months, Rosti had made $10,000. With that as bankroll he began to play on Wall Street. "At the time it was not the same casino it is today. Then there were little crap games all along the street. My edge is that I knew the rules. Actually, I knew there were no rules, that everybody was crooked, the sellers and the buyers, and knowing that, I was able to make money. Because anytime I made any sort of profit at all, I got out." Occasionally he worked as a maître-d'hôtel or club manager, where his distinguished appearance and his cultured accents were highly rewarded assets.

Two or three days a week, he would go to the Public Library at Forty-second Street and would read very heady matter, works on logical positivism by G. E. Moore, Wittgenstein, and Lord Russell. He would have liked to practice philosophy, to be a philosopher, but in this country at that time that was no way to make a living. So life was pleasant. He was single. He had money. He lived in the Village. He drank and caroused. He read a lot and he worked a little. And then he met the prince.

In the months that followed the discussion at the cafeteria, Rosti ran into the prince a few times, and on these occasions His Highness embellished the tale of his reign. It seems that his parents died in mysterious circumstances out in Oklahoma and he was brought to the Lower East Side of New York to live with relatives. "My domicile was in the vicinity of Stanton Street," the prince recounted, "and I was sent to a private school, which, unfortunately, was run by a rabbi. The curriculum was not at all suited to my princely mission and therefore I had to have tutoring in literature, music, fencing, military science, and finance—gold, you know."

As the relationship of the emperor without seraglio and the philosopher with his honesty in the closet drew closer, the older man confided to his young friend that he had experienced difficulties in his early years. There was a time when he was reduced to working as a pants presser, but that had lasted only a brief period. Thrice he was incarcerated and thrown into prison in connection with the theft of jewels, and he languished in bleak cells for periods of up to two years. Actually, he told Rosti, he was innocent of the crimes, having been framed by agents of the Turkish mafia intent on besmirching his name and preventing him from finding the six thousand tons of gold that had been buried by his royal ancestors.

The plot was very complicated, involving a doppelgänger who had actually committed the crimes and who, except for a scimitar tattooed on his forearm, resembled the prince in every detail and mannerism. The police did not believe this. Instead, they thought the prince was a man named Gus Danowitz, who had a long-standing reputation for knowing his way around safes and jewels. At any rate, the prince's last incarceration had taken place three years previously. It had nothing to do with jewels but with the Junoesque red-headed painter who at the time was his wife. It was 1924, and the prince was hard at work as a painter of abstract canvases. It was a fairly flush time. His wife, Esther, had some money, and he was periodically employed as a mural painter and decorator of speakeasies. On a March night he had just put the finishing touches to a large titian-haired and naked wanton that he admired very much. After accepting the praise of the club's owners and patrons, and filled with the joy of creativity and the sin of pride, the prince returned to Esther, his wife, and, grabbing her by the hand, pulled her from her own work and dragged her to the club. "That is my masterpiece," the prince declaimed, pointing to the pneumatic nymph on the wall; "and this has been my model," he said, proudly holding his wife. Mrs. Courtenay was not happy. She turned her eyes from the picture and tried to leave. The prince grasped her arm firmly. "My wife with the magnificent red hair was constantly before me as I painted, as I put forth my love and admiration into the image. She was my model because her form and face never left my mind as I worked." Mrs. Courtenay broke away and raced out into the street, followed by the prince, who caught up with her on the street and knocked her down. The matter was brought to trial and the prince was sent to Welfare Island for a six-month term for wife-beating. What's more, his wife obtained an annulment.

It had been a turbulent marriage. She had left him two years earlier after a domestic fight involving the hurling of a steam iron. A kind old magistrate who said that he recognized that those were the ways of artists urged them to reconcile, and they did, leaving his courtroom arm in arm. A year later she left him again, after he had burned some of their furniture on the street. It seemed that while his wife was away visiting her family in upstate New York, the prince neglected to pay the rent on his studio. An eviction order was duly signed and City Marshal William J. Kelly came to enforce it. But the prince had no plans to resist. What he had plans for was an auto-da-fé. After first contacting reporters from all the newspapers in town, the prince neatly assembled his paintings in heaps on the sidewalk. "I'm flat broke," he said to the crowd drawn by the spectacle. "People here are too materialistic. They don't recognize genius or the spark of genius." Then he set the spark of fire to his works. "I'm burning them all up, and every artist in New York who has the same hard luck that I have, and there are many, ought to do the same thing. Look at these paintings. They are what I call impressionistic love poems. I tried to emphasize the principle of romance, mystery, and the poetry of life in my painting. That one there must be worth at least $500." At this point, Marshal Kelly, whose credentials as an art critic are unknown, intoned, "Well, if Woolworth was selling it for ten cents, I'd think they was profiteerin'." The artist either did not hear the remark or pretended not to. "This was my favorite, but I don't like any of the stuff now. I'm sick of the whole thing. No, I don't think I'm going to paint anymore." This episode led to the second crisis in the marriage. It recovered only to succumb to the third, the nude on the wall of the High Flying Club.

That was the end of domesticity. The prince resumed his peripatetic living style, residing in a succession of small hotels. He kept his papers and artist's materials at houses of friends so that when the inevitable eviction came and the hotel manager locked up his few belongings, he could buy a new toothbrush and try a new hotel. He once told Rosti that he had stolen a hotel room for a year. He had been given the room to live in while he painted a mural in the lobby. Then in the evenings he carefully constructed a canvas flat that fit over the door of the room and blended into the wall. The prince contended that the misappropriated chamber was discovered only when bookkeepers examined the records and found no rents had been collected for it, and a delegation was sent up to pound on walls and search for the room. As for food, when he had money, he bought it; when he didn't, others bought it for him. He could and would stand, in his spats and fancy cane, in front of a restaurant or cafeteria for hours. Eventually someone would strike up a conversation with him and eventually someone would buy him a meal in exchange for his conversation.

And this was the way he was living when he met Rosti. He rose at noon and would work on his painting, on his novel, *Rohan of the Year 20,000*, or on his poems. The novel, the manuscript of which contained more than five hundred pages, was written entirely in a code that no one has deciphered. His evenings were devoted to rambling, to cadging meals, and increasingly to meetings with the Roman philosopher. Two or three times a week the two would gather at the Sir Hubert or Rudleys and discuss plans for the restoration of the empire. Then they would withdraw to the Dome, where the prince would declaim some poetry, winding up the night at Princess Marie's, a whorehouse on MacDougal, or at some speakeasy on Bleecker Street.

It was in 1934, on June 1, that Rosti appeared for an appointment with his titled friend. He was to meet the prince at eight o'clock at Rudleys and so, quite naturally, he arrived at the appointed spot at ten. The prince had a notoriously undisciplined regard for time, despite his custom of wearing three watches. But at midnight His Highness had not turned up, so Rosti proceeded on his own, certain that his friend had found something better to do. The next morning he read the paper and found out what had happened. It seems that a stout and respectable violinist named Otto Krist, who played at Lüchow's famous restaurant and who was a classmate of Fritz Kreisler, reported to the police that his eighteen-year-old daughter, Louise, a student at a business college, had not returned home since the day before, when she had gone to a poetry reading at Washington Square Park. It did not take long for the police to learn that the prince was among those at the reading and that the young girl was with him later that evening at the apartment of a Madame Vrbovska, where a meeting of a poetry circle known as the Ravens was taking place. Among the others there was Jan O'Brien, a sister of the police commissioner. Another participant, Vincent Beltrone, whom the newspapers described as "artist, poet and fascist editor," told the investigating detectives that he had objected to the way the dapper, if not dashing, forty-eight-year-old prince was pressing his affections on the girl and had challenged him to a fight. When the prince declined, Beltrone offered to see the girl home. The girl declined, choosing instead to leave with her prince. That, the newspapers said, was the last anyone heard of the pair. Meanwhile, Rosti and a good bit of the population of New York read of the pleas of the good burgher Krist and of the police in regard to the search for the lovers.

Then on July 21 a patrolman, Joseph Gleason, spotted the couple as they walked hand in hand at Tenth Street and Third Avenue. He stopped them, and although they identified themselves as Mr. and Mrs. Robert White, took them to police headquarters. There the elder Krist, anguished and distraught, identified his pretty daughter, shouting at her, "What is the matter with you, are you crazy?" The young girl's response was to turn her back on her father with a flounce of her long braids. To the reporters who asked whether she knew of the prince's criminal record, she said, "Yes, I know all about him and I love him. I am willing to marry him." The prince was equally dignified, pledging undying fidelity and devotion to his young love. "This has been the perfect romance. I have been dreaming of this for ten years," he told the reporters, whose presence always heightened his performances. "She is a perfect pearl. If anything should separate us, I will kill myself. I cannot live without her. She is the answer to my prayer." Then, for the benefit of all, he recited his prayer: "I am the superior mind and the perfect original thinker. I am a genius. I am a force of the universe. The laws of the universe being in harmony with me, we the forces of the universe command that Louise Krist and Robert de Rohan Courtenay should successfully come out of their trouble and shall be married today."

After an appropriate pause, he turned to the amused reporters and onlookers and asked, "Perhaps you people could be moved to proffer us a love token of two dollars to cover the license, as we only have fifty cents between us."

18

The request was spurned. After this scene, the prince and his Louise were parted, she being charged as a juvenile runaway and he with seduction. They were led to separate cells, but not before the prince borrowed a pencil and dashed off a poem to his beloved. He did not give it to her, though. He gave it to the reporters.

The poem went like this:

Some time in the distant future
When you look back upon the sea of vanished time
And unseen petals of the rose that never bloomed
Fall slowly in the dark
Like saddest tears
The stillness of the abyss of love that was denied
Will be your rosary, my most adorable madonna.

For nearly a week the lovers languished while the courts deliberated. Louise underwent a psychiatric examination that found her to be sensitive, intelligent, and abundantly sane. She was released on probation in the custody of her parents. The judge further ruled that her release was conditional. She was not to marry the prince while still a minor and she was not to communicate with him for six months. Two days later the prince had the case against him dismissed, despite the arguments of Mrs. Charles A. Oberwager, a lawyer retained by the Krists. She told the court that her staff was searching files in Washington to determine whether the prince was an alien subject to deportation. There was no doubt that the good violinist wanted the prince way the hell out of the country. But the prince was ordered released, and at five o'clock on July 26 he strode out of the West Side court a free man. There to greet him were two thousand admirers who cheered happily as the little man moved among them. Some shouted,

"Love Conquers All," and one blushing girl rushed to him and handed over a bunch of roses, somewhat wilted in the afternoon heat. What would he do now? asked a young man. Would he contact the lovely Louise, now that she was sequestered from him by edict? "I don't know," he answered. "I have only three cents to my name."

But, as often happens, the decision on what next was not the prince's. The vicissitudes of history intervened in the form of two policemen armed with warrants for his arrest issued by the Department of Labor and charging him with violation of the immigration law. The papers were served on him at the apartment of a friend with whom he was staying. A search of the premises disclosed his total possessions to be a broken comb, a toothbrush, and a manuscript described by the detectives as being unintelligible. This was certainly *Rohan of the Year 20,000*, which its author maintained was an "erotic love story, greater in its imaginative quality than *The Arabian Nights*."

The cause of the arrest lay in Mrs. Oberwager's researches. A landing certificate had been found issued to Robert de Rohan Courtenay in 1917. The passenger had debarked at New York from Cuba, where, incidentally, the prince had indeed lived for a year, serving as a general in the Cuban Army. On the certificate Germany was listed as the place of birth. This indicated that the prince was an alien, and since he had a record of several felony convictions and since he had no meaningful employment, it could be argued that he was an undesirable alien and should be deported. Another problem was the business of the title. How could a citizen of this country lay claim to a foreign title? And how could he have been born in Guthrie, Oklahoma, in 1886, when the town did not come into existence until 1890? These were weighty problems, but they did not seem to bother the prince as he draped himself around the guardrail of the launch taking him to Ellis Island for deportation hearings. With straw hat held high against the New York skyline in jaunty salute, the prince posed for photographers, dashed off another poem, and, after saying that he expected to earn $50,000 in the forthcoming year from his poetry, declared that in the unlikely event his case should go against him, he would go to China, where his sweetheart Louise would follow. What happened from that point on remains obscure. The hearings were not open to the press, and all that was reported in the newspapers was that eight boxes of pencils had been used in taking down testimony. But then a month after he was taken to the hearing, he was brought back. There were some who believed that no country could be found to take the prince, but His Highness's own account was more involved.

"I knew from the start that the burden of proof lay with them," the prince once recounted as he sat with friends at the Fifty-seventh Street Automat. "They would have to prove that I was not born in Oklahoma, and I knew they couldn't do that. The landing card, well, that was damaging, but it could have been a mistake, a slip of the wrist, a clerical error, a momentary lapse of memory. Therefore I decided to build my defense on the concept of my royal legitimacy. I had several friends with some money and at my urging they were able to secure five trunkloads of books dealing with the history of the Byzantine Empire, which were then shipped to Ellis Island. When the government lawyers saw them, they quite naturally asked for an explanation. 'This,' I responded, 'is my evidence.'

" 'What kind of evidence?' the lawyers demanded.

" 'Evidence that I am who I say I am, the heir to Byzantium.'

"Of course, the prosecution objected. But the hearing

examiner relented. He saw after all that this was the key to the case. If I am the grand duke of Byzantium born in Oklahoma, then everything's jake and I can stay. If, on the other hand, I am not the grand duke, or if I am the grand duke born in Germany, then I must go. So I began reading my evidence. It was glorious stuff, Latin, Greek, French, and English. Actually, the real books were just in half of the first trunk; the rest of the boxes were filled with the Hardy Boys and copies of *Collier's* and *The Saturday Evening Post*. The prosecution, of course, objected when I started reading Latin, but I patiently explained that that was what was spoken in the early years of the empire. My brilliant defense ran on for several days and I was in a position to have it run on for a couple of months, but I was interrupted by the examiner who, after consultation with the prosecution, terminated the proceedings as a savings to the state."

Whatever the legal rationale may have been, the prince did return to Manhattan to resume his quest for the throne of Byzantium. The romance with Louise lapsed and the diminutive noble continued to cadge meals and sleeping quarters while turning his attention to pling plong, which he described as a poetical form that delved into "man's pre-primitive subconscious. This," he went on, "is the new surrealistic literary medium for creative expression. Its sounds are fragments of the original source of all language. It takes talent to bring them out. I have that talent." Never encumbered by modesty, the prince had great hopes for his new mode, promoting it in coffeehouses where he would declaim to startled audiences. The only publication to have accepted any pling plong was the *Bowery News*. The prince was dismayed by the public's apathy. "This country just does not understand chivalry, aristocracy, poetry, or talent. Listen to this. If there were any justice, this poem should bring me $25,000, but there is no justice and I have trouble even giving it away." Then he read one of his favorite pling plongs, called "My Beautiful Rag Doll."

And in the moonbeams tender drifting
While all the poontalong was shifting
I kissed her softly sikibifting
My Beautiful Rag Doll
Param Parang lolipoona sorny
Peeliseesee, karinta, porny
Rapentidee, boloo, fahtorny
My Beautiful Rag Doll.

He read it one night at the Dome, and a man stood up to ask what it meant. "It doesn't mean anything," said the prince with great dignity, "it just is." With that he launched on an extemporaneous explication of the creative process and told the yahoos how he came to be visited by the muse Euterpe and so was propelled into the poetry business. "I used to do a little crap shooting, but I gave it up because of the greed on the faces of the players. Besides, the night I threw seven sevens in a row, the party next to me began fiddling with a large shiv. 'My boy,' I said as I headed for the door, 'that was just a demonstration of mind over matter without concern for personal gain. I willed those naturals. You could do it too.' I never threw those bones again, and now I write poetry." It was less dangerous, but less lucrative.

The 1940s and early '50s were bad times for the prince. Except for Rosti there were not too many of the old friends around. He stalked the Automat and told his stories, but the sense of exhilaration and gusto was gone. Two or three regulars could be counted on for meals, but it was a recession in the Bohemian business. Things got so bad that the prince actually went to work for the first and only time in his adult life. Every day he would put in a casual appearance at the office of a shipyard where he was employed as secretary to the superintendent. His employer was a kindly man and an old friend and he allowed the prince great latitude. Meaning that the prince would come in at three in the afternoon and leave at five. He would spend his time meticulously polishing his shoes, and shaping his beard and mustache, which by this time had flourished into a Victor Emmanuel growth. This period, which was the artistic nadir of the prince's long life, lasted until the mid-fifties, when he qualified for relief, quit his job, moved into the cell he called the "Jade Palace," and stepped up his campaign to be crowned. It was at about this time that Rosti, too, found himself with more free time, and what had been a friendship between the two men blossomed into a full-scale partnership.

It was at the Whaler Bar that the two began talking one day of the quest. The prince noted with some dismay that he was getting old and that perhaps his lifelong goal was slipping from his grasp. The conversation shifted to the state of the economy, and Rosti observed that he had been reading of the gold drain. And then both men stopped talking, realizing that they had hit upon something of momentous portent. "My God, what a catastrophe," said the prince. "Without gold how can people eat, how can they sleep, how can they make love?"

"Exactly," said Rosti.

"And here I sit, knowing the approximate location of the six thousand tons of buried Byzantium gold, powerless to help."

And then the idea that had been gestating in both their minds was given expression by Rosti. This, he said, was the answer. The prince would wage a campaign for the support of the United States. Washington would recognize his claim. He would claim the gold, and then he would turn it over to the United States to be used to bolster the dwindling stocks in Fort Knox.

"Exactly," said the prince, and raising his glass of Pouilly-Fuissé, proclaimed Rosti his Maître de la Cour. "Here's to the Grand Illusion," he declared.

And so the campaign started. Letters were written to President Eisenhower, to the governments of Turkey and Bulgaria, and to Dag Hammarskjöld. Most of these luminaries acknowledged receipt of the messages, and their very nice letters are now part of the prince's archives stashed away in Rosti's apartment. "We were having a great time," said Rosti, "but we really weren't getting anywhere until one evening at the Fifty-seventh Street Automat the prince berated me. 'Look,' he said, 'Ford has foundations, Rockefeller has foundations, but I, heir to all Byzantium, have none. Go get me some foundations.' "

Rosti saw immediately how right his liege was and went to work drawing up plans for an eleemosynary foundation that would capture the imagination of the country and project the prince into the hearts and minds of all Americans. Four days later he reported back. "Your Majesty, as you may be aware, the papers are presently full of outer space. Everyone is excited about it. They know it is there but they don't know what to do with it. The same, I have determined, is true of garbage. I propose that you underwrite a foundation that will encourage the study of the ways that garbage and rubbish can be transported to outer space."

After a significant pause for consideration, the prince rejected the idea, saying that it was probably good enough for his second foundation, but that something grander was needed for the prime venture, and again Rosti thought, returning a week later with a proposal for the American Foundation for the Happiness of Bulls. The prospectus for this venture, as written in the name of the prince, read as follows:

> For economic reasons, the experts have resorted to the unromantic, but profitable scheme of using artificially heated dummy cows to seduce prize bulls highly valued for their semen. This is then put into test tubes and sold to farmers and breeders of prize livestock. The process goes under the vulgar term of artificial conception or insemination. Now what is the outcome of all this? The bulls are unhappy because they haven't had the cows, the cows are unhappy because they haven't had the bulls. If the bulls are unhappy then no one cares except themselves, but if the cows are unhappy, they don't give milk. If they don't give milk, the farmers are unhappy. This is economics and the farmers understand economics. But not love. Therefore the farmers inject other things into the cow, vitamins and chemicals, which make them give milk. So now the cows give milk, but it is not the milk of contented cows. It is artificially conceived milk. Babies drink the milk and, of course, they grow up to become beatniks.

In these circumstances, Rosti advised the prince to establish a foundation that would provide the cost of transportation of a real bull to any cow that wanted one. This idea was immediately approved by the prince, who composed a proclamation that said: "The scientific bamboozling of bulls and cows out of their most pleasurable activities, together with the complete vulgarization and decay of their love affairs, is rapidly spreading in the U.S.A. and U.S.S.R. As my subjects know, I love the way things are done among the flowers, the birds and the bees, and I am convinced that our monkeying around with them will, sooner or later, add nothing but chaos and destruction to the race." So it was decided. Stationery was printed up and the matter was brought to the attention of the clientele of the automat and other select gathering spots. And what then? "Well," said Lord Rosti, "once we were tax-exempt, and achieved our primary objective of setting up foundations, we let the matter rest."

Other matters, however, were pursued. Letters were sent out in search of a long-tailed cock, and the prince appeared on *The Steve Allen Show* to state his case. Later he appeared on other shows, and Lord Rosti continued pressing and scheming until he was temporarily sidetracked by his involvement in the coffee business. It was 1958, and Lord Harry and the prince were eating at the Jumble Shop on Eighth Street when a rich Texan, intrigued by the prince's unusual costume and mustache, struck up a conversation with the pair. The Texan berated artists for their condescension toward men of business and said that making money was not so easy. The prince took himself out of the conversation completely, thinking it vulgar. But Rosti was amused and noted that he had better things to do with his time than make money. Actually, he had done all right making money. The Texan then offered a challenge. Why didn't Rosti try to start a business from scratch and see if he couldn't make even $10,000 in the first year? The Texan said he would even offer a prize if Rosti could do it, say $100. "It was an interesting proposition and I decided to take him up on it." He walked around the Village until he came to an Italian delicatessen owned by a friend. There in the window were small imported espresso coffee makers being sold for $3.95. They gave Rosti an idea. He asked the owner how many of the machines he could sell him for $5.95 each. The owner replied in wonder, "What, are you crazy, I can sell you all you want for $3.95, what the hell you want them for at $5.95?" "Because," replied the man who had kept his honesty in the closet, "I'm going to sell them for $15." The delicatessen owner looked at his friend as if he were insane. "I can't sell them at $3.95 and you want to sell them at $15? You are crazy."

"I told him he didn't understand business. Anyway, he agreed to sell them to me. Next I put an ad in the Sunday *New York Times* for imported coffee makers for espresso coffee for $15. The first week, I got 150 orders. I wrote back to some of the people that wrote and asked them why they bought the machine. All the answers said the same thing: We don't care about espresso, but we do want a better cup of coffee. So I went into the coffee business."

He went to a roaster on Cortlandt Street and asked the man to prepare a good blend. Coffee, generally, was at that time selling for forty-two cents a pound. Then he had special envelopes printed up with the name Avatar, which means "the incarnation of a deity." Under the brand name was the legend "the coffee of the Gods." The envelopes were made to hold a quarter of a pound, and part of Rosti's merchandising campaign centered on the claim that since there was less in each package it would stay fresh longer. He says now that that may be true. The other part of the campaign was the price of the product. He took his first bags to the Greenwich Village delicatessen and asked his friend to put them in the window with a sign that said: "This is the best coffee in the world. Because it is the best coffee in the world it costs $1 a pound. But do not risk $1. Buy a quarter of a pound for 25 cents." The message worked and the first shipment was quickly sold out. Lord Rosti continued to buy his coffee on Cortlandt Street, package it into bags in a MacDougal Street basement, and put it into stores. Fifth Avenue specialty shops started to sell it, and Clementine Paddleford, the food editor of the *Herald-Tribune*, came to interview the coffee merchant. "That was what did it. I told her I got the recipe for the blend from my father, who was the personal chef to Pope Pius XI, and that he had gotten it from his grandfather, who in turn had gotten it from a manuscript attributed to Rousseau. I told her that my pet parrot was my book-keeper, and I served her a cup of coffee into which I had put a Benzedrine. Naturally, she thought it was a very happy cup of coffee." Whatever Miss Paddleford may have actually thought, she returned to write a column-long story about the one-man coffee merchant, promoter, and salesman. She omitted the part about the parrot and the business about his grandfather, but Rousseau was mentioned and she did say it was very good coffee. "I made $50,000 that year and then got out when everybody else's coffee started to go up. I didn't think I could sell it for $2.00 a pound." That was the last period of prolonged work for Lord Rosti. He recently got married at the age of sixty-five, and he still goes to the library several times a week. He still promotes the existential community and is now thinking of creating and circulating a monthly national hypocrisy index that would graph the fluctuations in cant, using a base year of 1945. Until the prince's death, he was also occupied with the coronation plans.

It was when the prince was eighty-two that he announced that he felt the time was drawing near for him to don the crown. The first order of business was the cock whose crowing was predicted by the Mexican priest. At the American Museum of Natural History, Lord Rosti was told that a bird with such long-tail plumage did exist. It was called the Coq Argenteuil and it was very rare, though the emperor of Japan had some. He wrote to Tokyo, explaining the situation and asking if the bird could be borrowed.

No reply was received, but within two months Lord Rosti was visited by a gray-haired and gray-suited man who showed him the letter and asked if he had written it. The visitor said he was from the United States government and had been asked to look into it by the Japanese embassy. "I told him the whole story and he left. I called a friend of mine who was supposed to know the Mafia, and I suggested to him that maybe a helicopter could be used to steal one of the birds from the estate of a collector on Long Island, but nothing came of that.

"Finally I got in touch with a rabbi from Vineland, New Jersey, where they have chicken farms, and he was able to get us a bird with a long tail, not exactly ten feet, but maybe twelve inches. That took care of the bird, but we still had to get the gown. What we needed was a mantle of a precise shade of purple. The dye for this is made by extracting the blood of the *Conquilia acoposa*, an insect of the Middle East which is not allowed in here because it brings infection. So I wrote to DuPont to see if they could make a synthetic, because, I explained, without it we couldn't get the gold. They never answered."

Some purple material of a very approximate shade was found, and a mantle was sewn. The coronation was held. It took place at the Cheetah. A rock band played and Andy Warhol came with his entourage. The prince was a bit dazed but exuberant. He flirted with the miniskirted girls, patting and pinching genteelly. He was happy: the dream had fruited. The lights dimmed and a blue spotlight beamed on the tiny old man. Three pretty girls stood around him as he placed the rhinestone crown on his head. The cock, coaxed and prodded by Lord Rosti, crowed. The prince was emperor.

Already the gears were turning for the next stage. Rosti was writing to U Thant. Permission would be sought to address the United Nations. The emperor would sponsor a party to retrieve his lost gold. The money would be turned over to the United States to stop the gold drain and to support artists. That was the plan. What happened to it?

"What happened? The guy died on me," said the director of the Grand Illusion.

Where Else Can You Go and Have Such a Good Time for Only $20 a Couple?

Rochdale Village looks like a kindergarten city built of blocks, its twenty identical fourteen-story buildings rising in homage to the right angle on a 120-acre site in Queens, where the old Jamaica racetrack used to stand. Instead of architectural frivolity there is plain sensible value, large apartments for reasonable prices. The 5,860 apartments are tenanted by working people with an average per-family income of about $12,000 a year. The place, which is a cooperative, is named after an early cooperative society founded in 1844 near Manchester, but the New York inflection turns the *Roch* as in *posh* into *roach* as in *roach,* something of a public relations setback for a city where the Blattidae creep and crawl in silent multitudes.

Back in 1963, when Rochdale was being built, black and white civil rights activists picketed and lay down in front of bulldozers to protest discrimination in the building trades. Now about a third of the residents are black, and some sociologists say that Rochdale represents the hope that integration can be functional. Others point out pessimistically that while the apartment houses are occupied by both black and white, the social institutions that have grown up around the complex have maintained racial and ethnic identities. These organizations include predominantly white or predominantly black weight-watching clubs, golden age societies, bowling leagues, dramatic clubs, a chorus, and woodworking and art shops. There is also the Muck 'n' Futch Mystery Club, a collective of some thirty couples that is now four years old. Its members, all residents of Rochdale and all white, include several public school teachers, a chemist, a cab driver, a glazier, a window dresser, a lawyer, a police sergeant, and a probationary officer. The club exists to provide fun and entertainment. Once every three months the couples gather for an escapade planned by a host pair. This husband and wife team collects $20 from each couple and uses the funds to arrange a night out. Under the bylaws the evening must include at least one drink and a meal. Beyond this the only limits are the imaginations of the planners and the budget. The hosts must spend everything they collect. They cannot reveal what is in store for the revelers beforehand, and they must serve as guides on the night of the mystery excursion.

On one spring night, it fell to Sybil and Bart LaVine to plan the outing. Bart is a thirty-two-year-old electrician and Sybil is a medical assistant working for a Negro doctor at Rochdale's medical facility. They have three children and have lived in the complex for five years. The couple had been in the club for only a year and had themselves been on only three trips, so they enlisted the help of their good friends Irving and Betty Gold in planning the adventure.

"We wanted to do something interesting, something unusual, but I'll tell you, it was hard," said Irving, a short, energetic man who is a shop teacher at a vocational high school. "Boy, this club has done just about everything already; you name it and we've done it." The problems, Betty explained, were further complicated by the fact that only twenty-one of the club's couples could come on the May night in question, thus providing the tour leaders with a working budget of $420.

"Boy, I'm telling you, we sweated this one," said Bart, a strapping and easygoing fellow. "We spent every weekend for the three months either at my house or at Irv's going over this thing, setting it up. It was like a military operation."

At any rate, the money was collected, and some two weeks before the departure date each of the members of the club received a cryptic note that was composed by the two couples and run off by Irv on his school's mimeograph machine.

The note said:

Did you know:
Hickory Dickory Dock,
The mouse ran up the clock.
The clock struck 8
So don't be late
At Rochdale Mall, we'll meet,
And Helen suggests you eat.

It was said that:
Old King Cole

Was a merry old soul
And a merry old soul was he,
He called for: an empty coffee can,
a flashlight (workable), an umbrella, and
something to write for thee.

Can you believe:
Old Mother Hubbard
Went to her cupboard
To get out her attire,
But when she got there
her cupboard was bare,
and all she could find
was some casual wear
(slacks for the girls, no ties for the men).

Did you hear:
Little Jack Horner
Sat in the corner
Eating his Xmas cake.
He put in his thumb
And didn't he look dumb
Cause it was time for his coffee break.

Elsewhere on the broadside, which was labeled "Gossip
Sheet," was an appeal to members to contribute $10 as a
deposit for the group's next outing in September. And
there was another reference to the mysterious Helen:
"Helen of Troy has nothing on Our Helen."

Then a week later came another shorter and clearer
note. This was a correction. The group was to meet by the
pond in Brookville Park, a grassy area some one and a half
miles from the Rochdale complex. Everything else still
held.

At the appointed time and the appointed place the ap-

pointed people began to arrive. As noisy jets on ap-
proaches to Kennedy Airport came in at the rate of one a
minute, cars drew up to the curb at parkside in more hap-
hazard formation. From them emerged women in slacks
and men in sweaters or Banlon shirts. Eleven of the
women had dyed hair. The youngest couples appeared to
be in their early twenties, and the oldest pairs seemed to be
in their mid-fifties.

They were greeted by Betty and Sybil, who, with their
husbands, had arrived well in advance of the others.
"Okay, bring on Helen," shouted one of the men as Betty
handed him an envelope and asked him not to open it
until all the members had arrived and received their instructions. The group broke into clusters, and conversation centered on baseball games and bowling leagues. One
short man with a beard said he had just come out of the
synagogue, where he had spent the whole day. "Gee, I'm
glad it didn't rain," said another. "Me too," said Betty;
"we won't need the umbrellas."

They talked about the planes streaming overhead and
wondered whether the people living in the houses across
from the park ever got used to the noise, and they guessed
that real estate values must have tumbled in direct propor-
tion to the decibel rise of modern aircraft. Then when all
the assemblage had been checked in with Sybil, she blew a
whistle and asked the couples to open their envelopes
carefully.

Inside each was a slip of paper and a coffee bean
painted either white, yellow, red, or blue. The note explained that similar beans were planted in the area of the
park next to the duck pond and that each couple was to
comb through the grass picking up as many beans of their
color as they could. "When you come across another-
colored bean, you are to throw it into the lake. You can

start now, but you have to stop when I blow the whistle."

The group moved down to the area where fat ducks were waddling, and there the first sighting was made. Then, for the next few minutes, the birds were joined by waddling people, some giggling, others serious, sifting the grass for coffee beans.

"What are you doing?" asked two kids, about ten years old, who walked by. "We're looking for coffee beans," they were told. Ralph Goodman, the police sergeant, impressed the children into his search for blue beans. With their aid, he and his wife, Sandra, collected 251 blue beans, more than anyone else, and consequently won a breakfast coffee mug.

While the search was going on in the twilight, Irving and Bart got out their Polaroid cameras and started taking dorsal views of the scavengers. "I got you, I got you!" shouted Bart, laughing, after snapping the yellow-slacked ample posterior of one of the women coffee-pickers.

"What kind of coffee is this?" shouted one man.

"Colombian coffee, you fool, and I'm Juan Valdez."

"I'm El Exigente, and I think it's undrinkable."

"It's not coffee at all, it's painted bird shit."

Betty blew the whistle. The next stage was on. The cars were to follow each other, but in the event they got lost they were to open yet other envelopes giving the next destination, which turned out to be the parking lot of a large shopping center near the boundary of Queens and Nassau County. A bus was waiting there, and the group left their cars to board it.

The bus took off, heading into darkness and Long Island. Sybil shouted over the conversations and asked people to count the beans they had collected. She gave a slip of paper to each. But a number of the men decided it would be more fun to throw the beans. The barrage began from the back. "Savages, savages," shouted Irving Gold in a high-pitched voice. An attacking party of four came up from the back heaving the beans, which hit some of the front riders in the necks. "Savages, savages," screamed Irving again, but this time he reached into a large bag of unpainted beans and flung handfuls at the guerrilla group. A solitary scout then raced down and shoved a bunch of beans down the shirt of the man who had spent the day in the synagogue.

"You son of a bitch," said the bearded man, laughing and wriggling to his feet. The beans slithered down and into his pants. He rose and undid his belt. "Take it off, take it off!" someone shouted. "No!" said his wife. "Look, I've got to get the beans out of my pants," he said, laughing. "It isn't just the beans that are going to fall out!" came a voice from the rear.

"This is a kind of a tradition," Bart explained to a couple who had never been on one of the outings before. "Last time it was peanut shells; they're always throwing something."

"Hey, Bart, can't you get a clean bus? This one is a mess, look at all the coffee beans all over the place," came a man's voice from the rear.

A small, middle-aged lady shouted, "Hey, save the beans, you can throw them at Helen." She seemed to want the barrage to stop, but she didn't really want to interrupt anyone's fun. Sybil kept asking people to count their beans, and at least half the couples were busy tabulating. "Watch out, don't hit the driver," she said. The driver kept his eyes on the road and didn't say anything.

The bus passed roadside stores that sold aluminum siding, Italian restaurants bathed in neon, used-car lots, and nineteen-cent hamburger hostels. It was heading for Mineola. Inside, a scrapbook containing photos and me-

mentos of previous trips were being passed around. It contained old invitations, party favors, and the Polaroid depictions of past raillery. It had things like a small business card that read: "M & F MYSTERY CLUB—MUCK 'N' FUTCH CHAPTER—MEMBERSHIT CARD." Beneath this heading in smaller type was the inscription: "Keep this card if there is any chance of screwing you tonight. If not, please return this card, I have other prospects to see."

Mrs. Gold pointed to a set of pictures. "This was the last one we planned and we thought we might even have some trouble with the law. We arranged with this stripper to be out on the highway. It was a dark road past some cemetery, and the bus came up and there was this woman next to a disabled car. The bus driver stopped, and the next thing this woman got on. She carried a portable record player with her, and he had blankets to put up over the windows. Then without anything—no word or anything—she plays the music and starts stripping. It was a scream. Then, to cap it off," said Mrs. Gold, "she got her period right in the middle of her act."

She showed other pages and other mysteries. There was the séance the group attended, and the evening they spent in a pool hall. One night there was a fairly formal dinner. And another time they began at Studio A, where the men, and some of the women, painted designs on the bodies of naked girls. Their creativity was documented in Polaroid prints. From there they went to Greenwich Village for a drink at a cabaret, where more peanut shells were thrown, and finally the whole group ended up in Chinatown for a late dinner. "Where else can you have that kind of a time for only $20 a couple?" said Mrs. Gold. "You know, if you go out alone with your husband, it has to cost you $20 just to see a movie, have a pizza, and pay the baby-sitter.

"We were a little hard pressed for what we wanted to do

tonight. We were almost going to go to another séance, but I didn't want any repeats. Because we were a little short on the money we couldn't have the bus for the whole night, and that's why we had that coffee bean hunt."

"I was doing some work on the piers," said Bart LaVine. "Some of my equipment—wire and stuff—was stolen. I told them about it and they said, 'Here, take two twenty-five-pound bags of coffee.' Well, we had all this coffee, and that's how we got the idea for the hunt. We stayed up a couple of nights laying the beans out on newspaper and spraying them with paint. Boy, I'm telling you, we worked on this thing, but it's really going to be great."

About this time the bus pulled to a stop on a major commercial street in Mineola. The stores were all closed. Sybil and Betty led the file down the street past a super-market. "Heed the signs," she shouted. "You're going to be tested on the specials." Then she paraded the group across the street, past a darkened lighting-fixtures store, an all-night pancake house, and then a florist's, where there was a black alley leading off the street. Up the alley came the oohs and ahs. "Where are we going?" "What is this?" "Helen's probably waiting."

In the middle of the alley was a small shed, and into this structure traipsed Betty and her charges. Inside was a wooden floor, lined with folding bridge chairs. On the walls were instructions for various judo and karate exer-cises, as well as a poster advertising an exhibition of the martial arts.

At the front was a short, squat, double-breasted sort of man, with glasses and a key chain, who greeted the arrivals from an improvised stage area. He was aided by a white-haired, motherly assistant, whom everyone assumed to be his wife.

The man identified himself as Lee George, a hypnotist.

"But," he said, "I'm not going to do any hypnosis tonight. Your very kind and dear hosts went to great pains to obtain for you the most unusual kind of entertainment. When they contacted me they told me that this was a very sophisticated group, and that you have seen everything and done everything and that they wanted something very unusual. So what I have prepared tonight is a show in which you, the audience, will be the entertainers. You probably don't know exactly how talented you are."

The first act of audience participation involved wine tasting. Mr. George's assistant brought out a tray with several bottles of cheap wine. He announced that the ability to distinguish between vintages took a great deal of talent. He was going to demonstrate how easily members of the audience could develop this ability, and he drafted three men. Pointing to one, he said, "I can see this man is a connoisseur."

"He's not a connoisseur, he's a kind of sewer," shouted one of the draftee's buddies.

The three were then blindfolded, and clothespins were placed on their noses. After that the trays were switched and, instead of wine, quinine water was poured into the tasting cups. "Remember," said Mr. George, "before tasting this you have to swirl the cup before your nose to excite the organ."

"Forget it. The last time his organ was excited was a century ago," came a shout from the audience. Everyone laughed.

"Now your organs are excited, take some of the substance and swizzle it in your mouths. What does it taste like?"

The first man laughed and sputtered, "It tastes like piss!" "Yeah," shouted the thin man in the audience, "but whose?" There was more laughter.

The second taster sipped and said, "It tastes like some-one I once knew." And the third man, trying to top his companions, sputtered but could think of nothing to say.

The next round of tasting began with Mr. George show-ing a can of evaporated milk to the audience. The gesture was met with giggles and guffaws.

"Remember, boys, excite your organs," said the hypno-tist. "Now drink. What does it taste like?"

The first taster spit out his mouthful into the cup, laugh-ing more than gagging. "That's the first time I've seen any-one come from the mouth," said the same man who'd been doing most of the badgering.

"What kind of way is that to talk for a schoolteacher?" rejoined the taster.

The second man gave his judgment. "It tastes like a bar-ium enema."

"Since when did you ever drink a barium enema?" came the call from the chairs. "I don't know, but when I came in here I didn't have to take a shit." The laughter, as in most of the cases, was mostly baritone. The women tittered, smiled, but did not look embarrassed.

The final round of drinks was served. This time it was clam juice. The audience and the tasters were running out of genitourinary tract comparisons. "Say, Teddy, I taste better than that, don't I," shouted the schoolteacher. The act ended, there was good-natured applause, and the tast-ers, their blindfolds and nose clips removed, returned to their seats.

"The next part of the talent show," said Mr. George, "is an orchestra. Now every orchestra needs a leader, so will that man in the horn-rimmed glasses please come up." The man did and was outfitted with a mop wig and given a large pretzel stick to use as a baton.

"You can eat the pretzel if you want," said the impresario, "but I warn you, I buy them from a pervert down the street and I don't know what he uses them for." The conductor sniffs the pretzel in an exaggerated pantomime. Meanwhile five of the women are called up. One is given a tambourine, three get kazoos, and the last a duck call.

"Now, this orchestra is like any other. It is made up of bangers and blowers. And these girls look like they can bang and blow."

"She does, she does!" shouts the husband of one of the musicians.

"Anyway, let me tell you how to play the instruments," he says to the kazoo section. "You blow the big end, don't put your finger over the hole, and don't put your teeth on it. Now I want you to play the 'Blue Danube Waltz.' The bangers keep banging and the blowers blow, but at the end of the phrase, everybody stop and let the duck call come in."

"Da-*da*-da- da-*da*-," went the kazoos. "Thrup-thrup, thrup-thrup," went the duck call. The phrase was repeated four times. The conductor bowed. Everybody clapped and the musicians, taking their instruments with them as door prizes, returned to the audience.

Mr. George then told a story. It seems that as a hypnotist he is sometimes called upon to appear in court as an expert witness, and this was the case a few weeks past. The judge who presided did not, however, believe in hypnotism and called Mr. George to the bench, asking him to prove his credentials.

Certainly, said Mr. George; did the judge himself want to be hypnotized? No, the jurist responded, but let Mr. George demonstrate using the bailiff. The man was called over and put into a trance. He was told that his arm would have to be kept rigid and that he would not be able to put it down until the hypnotist snapped his fingers. In fact, the harder he tried to put it down, the more rigid it would become.

"Well, that's what happened. The judge told the bailiff to put his arm down, but he couldn't. 'Well, that's very interesting,' the judge told me. 'I wonder if we couldn't discuss this thing further in my chambers.' Well, you see, the judge was of a certain age and he had certain problems. You know people have problems. I can tell that none of you have these problems, but certain people have them. Well, I stayed in his chambers for a while, and then the judge came out into the court and said, 'Court's dismissed, and it's thirty days for contempt for anyone who snaps his fingers.' "

A few other acts were assembled by the maestro. In one, three men were selected to have theatrical beards pasted on their faces by three of the women. One of the subjects was made up to look like a Hassidic rabbi, another like a werewolf, and a third a Kentucky colonel. While the women pasted on tufts of hair, the audience howled. Sergeant Ralph Goodman got up from the audience to announce, "Why cultivate on your chins what grows wild on my ass?" There were prolonged howls.

Finally, a panel of three sex experts was assembled at the front of the room—two men and a woman. Mr. George said the group would answer any questions of a private nature thrown out by the audience. Almost all the questions were addressed to a large man with an overhanging belly who appeared to be in his late forties. "Tell me," one man asked, "when was the last time you saw your balls?"

"I use a mirror," the expert replied good-naturedly.

"How do you wash them in the shower?" the questioner continued.

"I take a bath."

The questions continued in that vein for a while until Mr. George said it was time for the heavyset man to "show his testimonials" since he seemed to know so much.

"You want to see my testimonials?" asked the man, who a few skits ago had gone into a small washroom, followed by Mr. George.

"Yes, let's see your testimonials."

The woman member of the panel shrieked a laugh and walked to the side of the room.

"Yeah, let's see his testimonials," shouted the audience.

"Okay, you want to see my testimonials," said the fat man, unzipping his fly. He reached in and withdrew a cotton cylinder, holding it out about six inches. "When I was born, it was this big." There was loud laughter. "When I was bar-mitzvahed, it was this big." He pulled out the cylinder another six inches.

There were more loud screams and laughter. The woman panel member was staggering, doubled over in laughter. "When I got out of high school, it was this big . . . then it was this big . . . and now it is this big."

As the laughter subsided, the clock at the front of the room showed exactly eleven o'clock. Mr. George thanked the audience, saying he was sure he had been entertained by its members more than they were entertained by him. He complimented them on their sophistication and turned the group over to the Golds and the LaVines, who shepherded the club back to the waiting bus.

Now there was some critical evaluation as the bus passed darkened suburban streets in Mineola, heading for the next unknown destination. "I thought Arnie did a great job as a wine taster." "When he took that thing out I nearly plotzed." And from the back of the bus, where a group of couples in their mid-twenties were congregated, came the repeated cry, "We want Helen!" Another pair explained to the new couple aboard that there was no place else "that you can have this kind of a time for only $20 a couple."

After forty-five minutes of driving, the bus passed a place called Helen's Bar and Grill and the alert passengers spotted it. "There it is!" they screamed. "That must be Helen." "Yeah, Helen of Troy," shouted another. "Helen, here we come."

The group debussed and trudged into the pleasant bar, which was filled with college kids who stared at the group as it filed into a large back room. "Have a nice time," said a pretty blond girl, smiling at the couples who paraded in, their name tags still attached to their lapels.

Tables were set up in the back with plates of potato chips and pretzels. Waiters came by for drink orders. "You can have whiskey sours, beer, or Coke," they said. The orders were taken and groups went into private conversations, waiting for what everyone knew would be the stripper. Fifteen minutes went by and the group was getting edgy. Anytime anyone walked into the back, there were shouts of "Take it off, take it off!" A woman went to the bathroom and a group chanted, "We know where you're going and what you're going to do."

Bart LaVine and Irving Gold were getting apprehensive. They went outside to wait for the entertainer. "Looks like we've been stood up," Irving said. "Goddamn it, after all the trouble we went to to get this place," said Bart. "We spent three weeks tracking down the owner and making arrangements."

As they waited out front, a woman with long red hair entered the place with a man and a poodle. "That must be her," said Betty Gold, telling her husband to ask her. "No, you're crazy, she wouldn't come into a place with a dog." They continued to wait. The woman with the poodle went to the bar. Half an hour later, after being badgered by their wives, Irving and Bart went up to the redhead and asked if she was Ginger. "Yes," she told them. "You see, you see, I knew it!" yelled Mrs. Gold. "Well, how the hell were we supposed to know that?" her husband replied. "What am I supposed to do, ask any woman who comes in here if she's going to take her clothes off?"

Word of the arrival spread quickly through the back room. The men peeked out to see what the entertainer—who was changing in a makeshift dressing room—looked like. "Wow, she's hung," was the verdict of one of them. A record player was set up on a small platform in the front of the room. A record of stripper music, heavy on the drum rolls, was put on.

The doors opened and the redhead, now wearing a floor-length, low-cut blue gown, strode in on high silver shoes. She marched about the room, smiling and waving.

"She likes you, I can see she really digs you," one of the younger men said to his wife. "Come over here to the end of the table where she can get at you." The wife slouched in her chair against the wall.

The performer then took off her gown. She did not do it by stages, or with mock coyness. She just unzipped it and took it off. There were no pasties, only the smallest of triangular patches covering her pudendum. She walked over to one of the men and squeezed her shapely breasts before his face. He leaned over and kissed each of her nipples.

She moved around the room, stopping here and there, rubbing her breasts in the faces and the hair of some of the men. At one point she stopped behind a woman who was talking across a table, paying no attention. The woman noticed something, turned around, and shouted "Oh!"

She came over to another man and, rubbing up against his face, reached down and pulled off the triangle. "She's a real redhead!" someone shouted. Some men took out their cameras. Ginger sauntered over to each in turn and softly and sweetly said, "Put that away, the cameras aren't part of the contract." She moved to a table and lay on her back, lifting her legs in the air. She went to one woman, leaned toward her, asking softly, "Don't you want to touch?" "No," said the woman, sounding worried. "Well, if you don't like it, why do you look at it?" Ginger whispered before continuing her rounds. As she hovered over a man who reached out to mouth her breasts, the man's wife hit him on the head with a coffee can. The wife was laughing, the man was laughing, and Ginger was laughing too. Then, about ten minutes after it began, Ginger picked up her gown, bowed, and strode out to some applause.

"Hey, I know that girl," said a heavyset club member. "I recognize her, that's Miss Cow Cunt of 1964."

The group was ushered out by the tour guides, and once again they boarded the bus. It was 1:30. "Boy, was she awful!" said one of the men. Others agreed. "She had a nice set of titties, but you could see the rest of her was beginning to go." "In two years she'll be doing eight-dollar tricks." "It's not a bad racket she has, she probably gets $50 and doesn't have to pay taxes on it for this kind of thing." "What do you mean she doesn't have to pay taxes, she's an entertainer." "Who knows she's working? She doesn't declare a thing."

One of the group, a self-styled student of pulchritude, observed that there was nothing sexy about the show. "I mean, Lily St. Cyr could get me screaming putting her clothes on, and I've seen strippers who just by taking their gloves off showed me more than that."

Bart and Irv said that the picture showed them by the booking agent must have been made ten years ago. "She looked a hell of a lot better in the picture."

The bus now pulled up to an Italian restaurant, where antipastos were set at tables reserved for the club. Forty-two servings of veal parmigiana were put out, with a large bottle of Coke for each table.

People ate and talked of what they were going to do tomorrow, of their bowling leagues and softball games. Sybil and Betty went to Ralph and Sandra and asked if they would plan September's outing. The couple said they'd be happy to, but would it be all right with everyone if they raised the per-couple cost to $25? Most people agreed. It would be okay. "I mean," said Ralph, "where can you go and have this kind of a time for even $25 a couple?"

Lemonade Artists and Cue Ball Kelly, the Finger Specialist

Gambling in New York is as ubiquitous as dog shit, and, on the whole, it is probably not so socially destructive. It is something like a seven-to-two proposition that the sanctified institutions of work and marriage have destroyed more lives than betting. Like drink, gambling has suffered from a bad press. There is some deficiency in our national character that leads us to measure sin by its excesses. The evils of drink certainly do exist, but who will speak for the countervailing benefits? Drink-crazed men do from time to time kill their spouses, neighbors, and landlords, and these acts are carefully recorded and reported. But where is the testimony to what must be the thousands of harried and desperate victims who, after miserable days of miserable work or miserable unemployment, struggle through the massed hordes and torpor of the subway and are dissuaded from hatcheting their wives by the fortuitous excessive imbibition of alcohol? How many potential rioters are too juiced for mayhem? I submit that having some of the people stoned some of the time can be a social benefit. So it is with gambling. There are, certainly, cases where bank tellers syphon off funds to restore betting losses. And there are those who bet and lose their rent money. But ranged against them are the hundreds of thousands whose lives are enriched by gambling even if they lose. People who can, through the risk of dollars, act out their secret dramas with no real great injury to anyone. These rituals are part of our culture, and groups that have formed around them exist in every part of the city.

In my time the first exposure came with the flipping of bubble-gum cards. Like most gambling games, this exercise in skill and luck is steeped in decorum and tradition. Once two flippers have decided to flip, one has to yell "Larry" before the other guy. This allows the first shouter to flip last. Sometimes the "Larries" are shouted simultaneously, leading to delicious arguments and interesting accommodations. In any case, the order having been established, the first player twirls his card in a sort of softball pitcher's delivery and the card, of course, lands either with the picture showing or with the tail up. It is now up to the second man to match the lie. If he does, he gets both cards; if he doesn't, the other guy wins. In my far from halcyon flipping days, it was my misfortune to come up against the slickest twirler on all the West Side, maybe in all Manhattan or even the world. This dumpy, short-sighted kid named Levine had started with a bankroll of maybe twenty doubles of people like Vern Stevens that his brother had once given him and had built it up into a collection that filled twelve shoe boxes. He had intuitively mastered enough basic aerodynamics to flip heads or tails at will. His release point never varied, but the speed of his downswing and his thumb pressure automatically compensated for wind velocity and density of atmosphere. To his mechanical proficiency he added psychological expertise, learning just when to goad and when to keep silent to get an opponent to risk his last few cards. He learned to dump, to lose on purpose and lull the other player into a false and soon-to-be-smashed confidence.

One of my first lessons in the transience of things came when this wunderkind returned from summer camp one fall and went the way of most wunderkinder. The magic was gone. His game was a shambles. Some said he had ruined it flipping on the soft ground of the country. Others said he must have grown a few inches and the ratio of his torso to his arm span had altered the perfect arc of his delivery.

At any rate, thus initiated, the city youth moves to new gambling pleasures. In the pre-computer age of my youth, junior high school brought with it such experiences as the three-player-six-hit parley, knucks, and pitching pennies. The first was a bet sponsored by some stripling entrepreneur. You could pick any three major league baseball players, and if between them they got six hits the next day, you would be paid off at odds of eleven to one. The usual bets were from a dime to a dollar. Knucks was a card game like blackjack, but instead of money the stakes were the right to slam down a deck of cards as hard as you could on the loser's fist. Sometimes knuckles would bleed, but you weren't supposed to cry. This not only advanced one's knowledge of mathematical probability, but also provided some structure for random sadism. Today there seems to me to be a lot less penny pitching around. Probably, because of inflation, a penny isn't worth the bother, and nickels may be a little too valuable. What the game may need is a good three-cent piece.

In addition to these purely gambling games, there was and is also a lot of betting on participation sports. There are still a few stickball teams in Red Hook that play games for an ante of ten dollars a man. And the glorious ethnic mix has broadened the scope of gaming. In Chinatown, for instance, there is a lottery called *boka-pu,* which, like everything else in Chinatown, is tremendously complex. Tickets are sold at prices ranging from a quarter to a dollar, and each ticket has something like thirty symbols. The buyer pays for each symbol he marks, and he is paid off in turn for each symbol that hits. The New York State Lottery, I am told, has not dented this action. A detective once told me that there are more than a million *boka-pu* plays a day, which seems ridiculous since that would mean that every man, woman, and child in Chinatown would have to make ten plays a day. But nobody has ever understood Chinatown. Dice games are played in private clubs in Harlem and also on the street. The Puerto Ricans have their own numbers bank. And the Dominicans and Haitians have brought their cockfights. They are held in basement storerooms, under tight security. The combating fowl are usually scraggly-looking white birds raised indoors and fitted with steel spurs. Cockfighting is illegal everywhere in the United States except in Arizona and Hawaii. But there are two publications devoted entirely to the sport of the breeding of birds. They give the results of contests on gentlemen's farms in Maryland, but they bring no news from the barrio.

Anyway, the point of all this is that a kid would have to be pretty catatonic not to realize by the time he is in high school that there is an awful lot of gambling around. He must know that the NO BETTING sign in his friendly neighborhood poolroom is just a harmless affectation like laws against masturbation. There are freshmen at Long Island University who win and lose as much as $50 a day—every day—in cafeteria pinochle games. There are kids who have to finish their homework in the afternoon so they can go to the trotters at night—every night. There are lunch-hour dice games, and there is hardly a large office building in Manhattan where somebody can't place a bet for you if you can't get to the track or to the Off-Track Betting bureau. There just may be more numbers players in the city than social security registrants. But it is the pool hall, smelling of smoke, chalk, and a trace of urine that is likely to be the city kid's first introduction to gambling as a way of life. It is usually a subterranean place, or tucked up above a smelly restaurant. And it is a male sanctuary, a place to hide acne pimples and block out bad thoughts. For most, it is a place you eventually leave, like college. For some, though, it is home.

Tony Pisano is thirty-eight years old and he has done many things. He has been married several times and he has owned and managed restaurants and bars. But four out of five nights a week, for the last twenty years, he has shot pool. Now he hangs out mostly in McGirr's, a classy establishment below Eighth Avenue where actors, hustlers, and gentleman players mix. You don't have to rack your own balls at McGirr's. Girls rush about setting up the triangles after the tables have been cleared. Tony, whom everyone there calls Tony the Sheik, is a gentle, well-spoken man who smiles a lot and likes to teach actors how to play. He taught Dustin Hoffman. He also hustles. One time, some years ago, he made $1,000 in a single night, but generally, he says, "if you take in $50, you're in good shape."

One night Tony the Sheik, who was just doodling around with his fine custom-made stick, pointed to a nearby table where a hustle was in process. A tall, blond man in a tweed sport jacket and horn-rimmed glasses was playing a short, middle-aged fellow, who moved around the table noisily and with animation. The short player was Jimmy the Greek, and the game he was playing was nine ball. At this point of the hustle Jimmy was winning with regularity. Earlier, Tony whispered, he had lost a couple. But even now the games were close and the Greek's shots would frequently brush the corner of a cushion before going in. Every ten minutes or so, as a game ended, the tall man would slide a $10 bill over to the Greek. The loser, or fish, was poised. Sometimes he would shake his head in anger at a missed shot. The Greek would respond with commiseration. "Tough luck," he'd say. Tony saw nothing wrong in the Greek's shooting form but he was a little more critical of his psychology, which, after all, is the key to the hustle. He thought Jimmy was being too hungry, moving too fast, and at this rate the fish would quit soon. Within a half hour the fish, who looked as if he might have been in town for a convention, said he had had enough and called for the tab. Tony figured that the Greek made off with about $120 of his money. As the tall man walked by him, Tony winked at his cluster of friends and asked, "What happened?" "I haven't played in a long time," the man answered without anger. "Well, if he was beating you like that, why did you stay so long?" said Tony in a sly ease. "You know, I thought I'd get my stroke back," said the stranger and left. "Look at that," said Tony. "They never really know, or they'll never admit to themselves, that they've been hustled."

Tony's reading of the fish was as follows: "This guy is not a bad pool shooter. He's here on business and he thought he'd come down for a little fun and he has been getting his kicks. But he just doesn't understand what's happened to his game. He could practice for a month and he'd still never beat the Greek, but he doesn't know that.

He figures he's just having a bad day, and that is true, but in his case any day he played the Greek he'd have a bad day."

Now that the fish had departed, the Greek was suddenly encircled by yapping creditors. Little old men who moments before seemed oblivious to what was taking place left their benches in the back of the room and swarmed to the victor, demanding money they had staked him to in recent memory. The Greek goes into an irate act. "What the hell are you all yelling about? What the hell do you think I won? It was just a crummy $60. See, look, here's all there is," and he grabs a fistful from his pockets, peeling off a $5 bill to give one $10 creditor. He settles a percentage of his debts. Tony whispers what everyone in the place knows. "I'll bet he's got another $60 in another pocket." The little old men go back to their benches to read racing sheets or doze, and Jimmy starts doodling around on a table. He is drawn into a discussion on the psychology of losers by Tony, who shows a great deal more bemusement and introspection than most of the hustling community. "There's some guys who want to lose," says the Sheik, who always plays in a black beret and looks something like a well-fed Basque smuggler. "Jersey Red, there was a guy who was as good a pool shooter as I've ever seen. He'd play for $500 stakes and he could be ahead $2,000. But he couldn't go to sleep while he was holding cash. He'd play and play until he lost it all. Then he'd go bum a dollar and sleep in the movies. If the poolroom closed before he could lose it, he'd play cards, craps, or anything until he tapped out." Tom Watkins, a regular but non-hustler, joins in. Tom thinks that there are some people like that, but he disagrees with Tony's view that poolroom life is neurotic and largely unhappy. "The tables are a better place to relax and there is more therapy here than in a bar. This is a male preserve. Sex doesn't come into it. It's all in the game and the roles are pretty well defined. You can take your beating and not lose friends." As for losers, the weirdest one that Tom knows about was Hal the Window Washer from Poughkeepsie. "He must have been crazy. Here was a guy who'd play anybody for anything. The word got out, and there was a regular shuttle up the Hudson. Guys were coming from Virginia and Chicago to take Hal's money. He resorted to burglary to keep up his game, and last I heard he was in jail."

"Action, that's all they know," said Tony with a touch of contempt. "Hell, it's all I know. But at least I got a job and make a living. A lot of these guys never work. Some of them will hack for a while, just long enough to put together a nut. If they're lucky, that will take them through a couple of months of playing. All of them are dreaming about a big score. They all know who took what from whom in the biggest hustles of all time. When the rooms close at two or three in the morning, they eat at Chinatown and go to sleep in rented rooms. Others who are still worked up head for the goulash joints and more action."

A goulash joint is an all-night cardroom. There is a string of these second-floor establishments down on the Lower East Side. The windows they show to whatever part of the outside world that cares to notice say ORIENTAL TEA ROOM. They are run by Albanians, and the game played is usually klaberjass, a Middle European form of poker. Unlike pool, where the flow of money can be kept to a minimum, the losses and winnings here are of coronary proportions. On any given morning at, say, 5 A.M. there'll be seven or eight bleary-eyed men, barely talking, just putting down cards and shoving heaps of money around. Fancy pinky rings are traded, and interspersed with the flashily dressed, gambling businessmen there'll be the exotic faces

of Orientals and even an occasional turbaned head. Everyone is very nervous. Once, when an innocent came up asking for coffee, there were nervous glances and men
reached for their pockets. But when the attendant finally
figured out that the wayward insomniac was not there to
hold up the game, the waiter just told him the place didn't
have any coffee. The thought that fixed the intruder as a
potential stickup man was based on the firm supposition
that the waiters knew all the cops. So who else could he
be?

But most confirmed pool players, says Tony, will gamble elsewhere but will save most of their energy and re-
sources for the tables. Many will get up around noon and
head for the brokerage houses. "It's sick," said the Sheik,
"but they'll just watch the tape. They like to see all that
money changing hands. If they do buy, it's strictly short
term, since they wouldn't want to tie up their nut. Like
they might pick up some stock in the morning and sell it in
the afternoon."

Most pool halls in the city are primarily places of relaxation and amusement, with most of the tables occupied by
kids who don't want to go to the movies. But there are others, like an all-night spot on Eighth Avenue and Fiftieth
Street, where pool is a business and where tables are
rented by the management like office space. This hall,
brightly lit, with new fast tables, has its own peculiar pat-
tern of money flow. At the bottom, feeding the economy,
are the pimps, mostly black, who hang around while their
stables work the area. They play and generally lose to
black hustlers, who in turn play white hustlers. The room,
which is up a flight of stairs that is strongly scented with
the piss of drunks, is a rough place. One autumn night a
man came charging up the stairs and smashed through the
swinging doors waving a pistol. "You guys think you are

going to rob me, but I'm going to rob you!" he shouted, and fired three shots into the ceiling. He lined up forty patrons and took their watches and money and left. The smell of gunsmoke had not cleared when all the tables were back in action. A skinny, chain-smoking young operative called Brooklyn Bucky had hidden in a wash closet during the holdup. The nervous, jerky youth had now come out to play and was laughing about the adventure. "Well, at least he didn't cut the cloth," harumphed Bucky, chalking his cue stick.

The crowd here is definitely not made up of boys playing but of men working. One, a short, stocky twenty-three-year-old, who dropped in just minutes after the shooting, is Jim Morgan. He is a Harvard graduate and was, at the time, working as a stock clerk at Macy's. After work he customarily put in hours at pool halls, mostly watching. Not for fun, but for profit. Jim, by his own admission, is not the greatest pool player in the world, an admission that is a great rarity in the hustle world, where self-promotion is as much an asset as a steady eye and a sure stroke. But he was good enough to finance his last year of college through a series of games with a rich classmate. In all he took about $1,500 from the sucker on the way to his diploma. He knows, however, that his talents are no match for New York's best shooters. What Jim does at pool halls is study players, assess players, tabulate their strengths and weaknesses, so that he can back winners in side bets. When the New York racetracks are open, he spends his days there, investing in the horse sense that he picked up in his native Virginia. At night he heads for one of several poolrooms, looking for a good bet. The purpose of the program is to put together a bankroll large enough to get him through medical school. According to his calculations, he should have the money in two years' time, having already realized and banked $2,000. The summer of his junior year, Jim said, he had a very successful time of pool hustling on the road. It is in this sort of traveling, to small towns, that money is to be made. The competition in New York is too fierce, although this is where the big reputations and the really big money can be made. What Jim did was to team up with an exceptionally good pool shooter from his hometown. The player was a hillbilly type, not Harvard material, but damn good with a cue. They took Jim's car and Jim's stake and started on a swing through West Virginia, Ohio, Missouri, Arkansas, and Oklahoma. Jim was the manager and the banker for his partner. "We'd stop at towns with one or two pool halls and work for our games." And then he explained how you do that. "Now, there's really a hundred forms, but essentially they follow one of two patterns. You can come into town shouting, 'I'm a tiger and I can eat any one of you chumps up.' That way you get the best player in town to put his reputation on the line, and maybe he can get some people to back him. Altogether they might come up with anywhere from $25 to $200 and you can knock it off in one quick shot. The other way is to come in quiet. Sit around and work for a game with a so-so player. You might just play for the time on the table. What you want to do is win, but by the smallest possible margin. From that point on you keep going after other guys, playing for ever larger stakes as the competition gets better. All along the way, you appear surprised at your own good fortune. Finally, you go after the king of the poolroom. It might take you three days to get there, but you've made money all along the line."

The key to any kind of a hustle is the lemonade, says Jim, and any other poolroom man will tell you the same thing. "Bring on the lemonade" means adopting any tactics that will hide your true speed, or give the opposition reason to believe they can best you. Lemonading is as important to hustling as public relations is to the pharmaceutical industry. Great lemonade artists are admired as much as, if not more than, great shooters. One whose name comes up in poolrooms from coast to coast is a legendary operator called Rags. His routine is to turn up in a strange poolroom, reeling and teetering, his clothes reeking of cheap wine, and dollar bills spilling from his pockets. The locals would practically line up to play him and he'd have no difficulty getting a game. But then, after perhaps losing a couple, he would sober miraculously. Rags, it seems, is a teetotaler, but before going out to work he would douse his clothes in muscatel. Another luminary was Pittsburgh Phil who had a collection of gas station attendant uniforms. He would come to play wearing one of them, with "Esso" on the back and "Phil" stitched above his vest pocket. The idea was to project the appearance of a man out for some harmless fun and relaxation. Actually, the uniform was fitting. He was a workingman working. One of the quaintest of the short-term lemonaders was Izzy, who squinted and read a Yiddish newspaper by holding it up to his nose as he sat in a poolroom. When he spotted a likely fish, he would approach the man holding up a half dollar and ask if the fellow had change of a quarter. Then, without too much difficulty, he would inveigle the man into a game. A variation of this ploy was worked by Angie the Fruit Man, who would feign simplemindedness, coming into the room eating a bunch of bananas.

In addition to such instantaneous ruses, there is the long-term lemonade, which is more complicated but can also be more rewarding. The idea here is to come into a fairly large-sized city like Holyoke, Massachusetts, and set up some sort of cover. The hustler may actually get a factory job. He wanders into a poolroom and sits around playing casually and establishing his mediocrity for all to see. Suddenly he gets lucky. Everyone knows he is playing better than his true speed. And because of vanity and cupidity, they all want to burst his bubble. His luck, they say, can't hold out. He gets cajoled into playing the better shooters. He feigns reluctance and wants odds. He keeps on winning, usually on the strength of some near-impossible shot. Within a week or two the hustler has beaten everyone around. Those who have lost to him introduce him to better players from other poolrooms, sometimes putting up the stakes themselves, feeling that the shark's luck will now certainly plummet and they will regain some of their losings. When all the sheep have been fleeced, the player quits his job and moves out of town.

In addition to the lemonade, the second major ritual of pool as a life-style is making games. What this involves is setting up handicaps. Two players who have a fairly accurate idea of each other's speeds will let it be known that they want to play each other, like the night that the Fat Man told the Truckdriver, "With a little bit of practice, and if you ever learn to take the pressure, you might turn into a half-ass shooter some day." There was no doubt among the spectators at the Golden Cue in Queens that what the Fat Man was saying was "I want to play you." The Truckdriver, in effect, accepted the challenge by rejoining, "The day you teach me anything, I'll take up knitting." During the next several hours, as both men sat around watching other games, they would periodically exchange cryptic insults. "What happened in the game with the Chinaman? You had him all the way until the end, then he broke you. You couldn't take the pressure. You better go back to driving trucks." And, "Fat Man, I get the feeling I'm going to have to reduce you to a couple of hundred pounds." All this is done with smiles and watched avidly by the regulars. What happens next is that one player will formally call the other's bravado into question. "All right, Fat Man, I'm ready. Twenty-five dollars says you walk out of here as thin as a cue stick." "You've got it, Truckdriver." And now the haggling gets serious. Who will break the pack? What game will they play? Perhaps one of them will spot the other a ball or two. In the case of the Fat Man and the Truckdriver, a few minutes of negotiations determined that they will play one-handed, that is with only one hand holding the stick. The first player to sink twenty-five balls will win. The Truckdriver will break, but he will receive credit for sinking two balls. Both the Fat Man, who eventually won, and his opponent are very good with just one hand. Others make a specialty of bank shots and like to play a game called pocket-apiece, in which each player gets one pocket and must make all his balls there.

Cue Ball Kelly, the impresario of the pool business, will play anyone in the world using his fingers instead of a cue stick. Cue Ball is seventy-three years old. He has a thickened body like Yogi Berra, a face like Jimmy Durante, and a voice like Joe Valachi. He is, he says, the "only guinea with a mick name that talks Jewish." Since he was twelve years old, he has spent something like a quarter of his waking life in poolrooms, with another large slice put in at racetracks. When he was younger, he put in long hours in front of a lasting machine, and he still claims the single-day record for putting shoes together—420 pairs in an eight-hour shift. For a while he ran a boxing gym, managed fighters, sold perfume. Now he is more or less retired. His son is grown and is a television executive. His wife is happy tending to the gardening in their suburban home, and Cue Ball is free to do what he wants to do. This means that every day after the horses stop running at Belmont or Aqueduct he turns up at the Golden Q, an air-conditioned airplane hangar of a poolroom in Queens. The tables have felts of red, yellow, and blue in addition to the traditional green. There are thick carpets on the floor, and in one corner there is a counter that serves sandwiches, coffee, and ice cream sodas. At several tables college boys play with their dates. It is a very different place from the three-table room in Flatbush where twelve-year-old Carl Zangale learned about human nature and the geometry of spheroids and rectangles. There was a keno board in that place, and card games went on in the back, and, as in many pool halls, you could get almost anything at a price if you didn't worry where it came from. Carl soon became Carlie and that in time gave way to Kelly. Cue Ball was a natural nickname and it became more natural when years later his hair fell out. When he was thirteen, his father once came into the place and dragged him out and beat the hell out of him. "I don't blame him," rasps Cue Ball. "I've been in poolrooms all my life. I've managed all the great shooters going back to Ralph Greenleaf—the greatest that ever lived; I've set up exhibitions and I've done a little bit of hustling, but I never caught my son in one of these joints— even now, I'd slap him pretty good. Pool players are all nuts, and pool halls are like houses for crazy people."

Even so, Cue Ball feels funny if he keeps away. He will not argue if you tell him he is like a resident psychiatrist at Matteawan Hospital for the Criminally Insane. He prefers to call himself the Ambassador, and a lot of people do. They point to the handouts he has given to broken-down hustlers, and to his work in popularizing and legitimizing the game so that now college boys can bring their dates to pool halls. But the fact remains that the Ambassador is a realist and he recognizes that his constituency is mad.

"Pool players are all psychos. They are crazier than horse players or cardplayers or anybody," he ruminates about his favorite subject. "I've buried more of them than I can count, and, before they died, I fed them when they were broken. I've watched them good. It's crazy, they live in their own dreams. A guy is perfectly normal outside, but he walks into a poolroom and it's like he's dreaming." He says he doesn't really know what "makes them go out of their heads." But he thinks "it's ego or something like that. All of them are saying that they're better than somebody else, all the goddamn time. I've seen dumb little pishers, who couldn't shoot their way through five hangers, go completely meshugener and start talking like they were the kings of the world. I've seen guys throw away careers and marriages because they think they can knock balls into holes better than other people. That's normal? It's got to do with manhood, too, like a sheriff in a Western movie, walking big because he's the fastest gun in Tombstone. But I guess what makes more guys crazy than anything else is the pressure. The pressure is fantastic. There's a guy I know can run off balls like a clock ticks minutes, but only when there's no money. You put up a nickel on him— not even his own money—and he cracks wide open and shakes like a leaf." Greenleaf was the only one Cue Ball knew who could live with pressure. For ten years he was unbeatable, like Babe Ruth, absolutely the greatest. He was drinking and had problems, but he could stand up to anybody. Greenleaf died on the eve of a match that Cue Ball had arranged for him. "He died broke like the rest of them, even though he made more money than anyone."

Cue Ball sees himself as unusual in two respects. For one thing, he is absolutely the greatest finger specialist in the game. And for the other, he is one of the very few sane people to have spent as much time as he has around pool tables and pool players. "Sure, I'm okay. Look, I don't even bet on any player. The last time I did that was twenty years ago. I put up $525 on a guy and he lost. You back somebody, you'll end up being put in the middle." This is a practice in which opposing players fix games and divide the money that has been bet and lost by backers. "You got to be crazy to bet on shooters. If they're not crazy, they're gonifs. I stick to horses, they're more predictable. Pool players, you see, are human." There is a lot of that kind of folk wisdom in pool halls.

What Cue Ball does now is to make a few bucks and advance the game through exhibitions and tournaments that he stages both in New York and throughout the country. The house sets up matches with players whom Cue Ball provides. In places like Pittsburgh and Syracuse, these matches can bring in as much as $20,000 a night in admissions. Cue Ball also referees some of the big tournaments in which he and the hillbilly players wear evening dress to bring tone to the sport. The tournaments, says Cue Ball, are all legit, but after the contests some of the boys "will do business." Exactly how business is being done at the upper levels of the sport is something very few people, and certainly not Internal Revenue agents, know for sure. There is a widely circulated, though unconfirmed, report that during one tension-filled afternoon down south a few years ago, a gentleman hustler from Virginia named Weenie Beenie took $87,000 from New Orleans Clio. It is part of the folklore that Minnesota Fats, who is really from the Bronx, made $200,000 in a single week in Norfolk, Virginia, as a sort of war profiteer. And Cue Ball says he knows of a guy who won nine oil wells from a Texas sucker. The highest-staked game he ever saw was a $15,000 pocket-apiece match that took less than half an hour.

The craziness of pool life is measured, says Cue Ball, by the twitches and shakes that players develop. But once he saw a different kind of vocational disability, and it sums up for him the weirdness of the life. It was in a joint up in Yonkers. The player at one of the tables was getting ready to break the pack. At the next table a young hustler was leaning over intently studying the lie of the balls. The first guy swung so hard that the cue ball caromed off the racked balls and went flying. It took one bounce and then flew into the mouth of the second player, knocking him out and breaking his teeth. "When he came to," says Cue Ball, "all he said was 'Thonofabitch.'"

Cue Ball has also lost his teeth, but it was through slow erosion, and it was this that led him to become the finger specialist. What happened, he explains, is that somehow the loss of his teeth resulted in the buildup of calcium deposits in his joints, which made it painful to swing a cue stick. It looked as if he would have to stop playing. But did deafness stop Beethoven? Cue Ball spent months developing his touch. He learned how to spin the cue ball into targets and how to put English on it. He also developed all kinds of trick shots, in which he spins the white ball around the table knocking all kinds of other balls into all kinds of pockets. Once a beer company, recognizing his dexterity, paid him $500 to put his hands on camera. In the right hand he gently held a pool ball. Below that, in his left hand, he held another, and between them a third ball spun suspended. A column of three balls. This is very hard to do, even though it looks easy. He tells people who tell him that it looks easy to try it, but he cautions them to wear shoes.

Romping and Stomping in a Most Righteous Manner

Chivalry lives on East Third Street, where the knights, Groover, Vinnie, and Jumpin' Jac, and their liege, Sandy, dwell in bonded communion behind a moat of garbage-strewn gutters. They and their eleven fellow Alien Nomads are motorcycle outlaws, living together in a tenement castle, extolling valor, loyalty, and their own kind of piety. But codes of honor are troublesome things. There was, for instance, the spring evening when two of the gang's mommas were standing on the stoop of the house at 77 East Third Street as two young black men were walking by. One of the men said something to one of the mommas. What he said, she said, was "What a girl like you needs is some good black cock." The Nomads are not particularly fond of blacks, and apparently vice versa. At any rate, the girl, one of those accorded the protection of the Nomads, approached the man, and either she hit him or he hit her or both. But it was in the middle of Nomad territory and soon enough a handful of bearded, earringed, tattooed

Visigoths who were in the ground-floor clubhouse came out and, as they say, wasted the mashers, who then went away.

But the thing about affairs of honor is that they escalate. An insult parried is an insult given. And so, as was fairly predictable, the blacks came back. It was a week later and this time there were fifteen of them. Tire irons and chains whistled and slashed, wielded by black and white combatants. Heads were split, blood was spilt, and fierce cries of "Get it on, motherfucker," rent the air. And when it was over, the Nomads were convinced they had won, repulsing the invading force from their street.

Now ten days had passed and Sandy, who is a handsome professional actor, circus aerialist, and veteran Marine sergeant with five years of active duty, was leaning against a railing talking to Jack of the Aliens' New Jersey chapter, an affiliated club. Two black men approached. About ten feet from the talking pair, one of them stopped, drew what Sandy said was a Magnum, and fired two shots that whizzed just past the leader's head and struck Jack in the back. Sandy chased after the assassin, joined in the pursuit by two patrolmen. The man got away. But the Aliens who were in the house raced out and grabbed his accomplice, who was turned over to the police. Jack was taken to Bellevue, where the bullets were removed from his back. All of this was disconcerting to the Nomads, but it was within their frame of reference. You do what you have to do to take care of things.

What happened next was not. No medical report, they say, was made of the incident at Bellevue. The alleged accomplice was taken to the local precinct and then released with no charges placed against him. And the very next day the police came and impounded the motorcycles of the club's members. These machines are beautiful, shiny chrome-and-black Harley Davidson 74s. They have been modified and rectified and polished and tuned to exquisite precision. They cost about $2,000 each and they are labored over daily for as long as eighteen hours. Taking a Nomad's motorcycle away is the worst thing you can do to him. The club members believe that the police action reflected a political decision. If warfare between the bikers and blacks appeared likely, the police, the Nomads felt, must have determined to come down hard on the bikers, since there are less of them than there are blacks. The plan seemed to be to harass the Nomads out of town. But Sandy is an intelligent and resolute leader and he held his people together. Even when they got their bikes back and were forced to reregister them and reinsure them and buy motorcycle helmets, and even when some of the members found that their beautiful machines had been ruined because while they were impounded someone had put sugar into the gas tanks, even then there was no thought of clearing out.

A word here about the political philosophy of the Nomads. They are patriotic. Next to loyalty to their brothers, and love of their machines, their strongest ties are to the United States of America, its flag and its symbols. "What we respect is the Constitution. We don't go around beating up on the citizens. That's not where it's at," Sandy once explained. "But if someone comes along and rides you and challenges you, there comes a point when your head explodes and you take care of it." Or as Jumpin' Jac says, "The hippies are coming around to doing their thing, but they're not together like we are. We understand that you can't be everybody's friend, the world's not built like that. People aren't ready for that. Somebody's going to mess with you and you've got to be ready to stand, alone or with your people, and fight for your rights."

As to being outlaws, they admit it. Sandy recalls that he was once in Disneyland, "and everywhere I went there I thought of my people. I saw the pirates and I thought of my people. I saw the old West and I thought of my people. You see, what we're doing is standing up for our right to live the way we want, and I guess that makes us outlaws." Then another of the Aliens, who were surging around their leader in the small communal kitchen, joined in. "Look," he said, "everybody's free to walk across the street when the light is green, but you're really not free unless you can walk across the street whenever the hell you want to. Of course, man, you've got to be ready to take the consequences." And Sandy took off on that. "That's the point. We don't mind taking the consequences for what we do. It's just that people look at us with our hair and beards and get scared before we get a chance to do anything. They'll come down on us, harassing and setting us up. That's what we have to put up with. Constant harassment. What we're doing is fighting for American individualism because, I'll tell you, they start taking away our rights, they start harassing us, and it doesn't stop. They'll come down on the straight people. Look what's happening in this country, blacks are fighting whites, old people are fighting young people, and if someone doesn't stand up for his right to be what he wants, everything's going to turn soft and communism will come in and take over and I don't ever want to see that happen." End of word about political philosophy.

The trouble with the blacks more or less died down, but new hassles took its place. Like the movie. Sandy got a contract for his gang to act in a movie in the late spring. It was to be a documentary about the club's outing to a beach in Brooklyn, a picnic with frolicking and fighting in the sand, and then more of the same back at the house.

The shooting script called for the Nomads and some of their friends from other Alien chapters to ride out, on about thirty machines, to a private beach near Sheepshead Bay. Now Sandy knew from past experience that anytime thirty cyclists rode out together in a pack, there would be sirens in no time and a lot of tickets and maybe even some arrests. When the group takes its runs up to Vermont and New Hampshire, Sandy carefully prepares an itinerary that he gives to a lawyer who then contacts all the police departments along the way to get permits and, in some cases, escorts. This time he contacted the mayor's office, and in due time he received accreditation good for one round trip to and from Gerritson's Beach. Even so, a dozen of the Aliens got tickets on the way out. Once there, the cameras started rolling and the Aliens started romping. Pretty soon a crowd of about five hundred kids gathered some two hundred yards away to watch the fun. Pretty soon after that a different crowd of about five hundred wahoos gathered to watch the kids watching the Nomads. And pretty soon, as the kids danced to the rock sounds on the beach, some people started calling other people degenerates. Now all through this the Nomads were separated from the crowd by hundreds of yards of sand and a wire fence. They just kept cavorting for each other and the cameras. But the crowd was pushing and shoving, and a small bunch of dummies decided to turn over a parked police car, which they did. Then there were a lot more cops and sirens and yelling, and finally the cops got rid of everybody. Then they came over to Sandy and told him to get his bikers off the beach. "Look, man, we had nothing to do with that," the police were told. "Maybe," replied the sergeant, "but your presence is inflammatory." The movie crew packed up, and the Aliens zoomed back to

Third Street. "Man, it was just more harassment," Sandy said.

And so the summer passed. The Aliens made a few runs up to land in Vermont owned by the Hell's Angels, the large West Coast gang with whom they were allied at the time. Actually, the Nomads were seeking to become full-fledged members of the Angels, and there were some discussions along these lines. In July and August, several Nomads were arrested for assault and freed on bail in connection with fights that originated in affronts to their honor. Two other members, Oats and Loser, came out of jail. Five men in civilian dress kicked down the door to the clubhouse one night. They had guns drawn and one bag of what might have been heroin. Another had a pistol tucked in his belt. They found only three people watching television. "There's too few, let's get out," one of them said. From their description, the gang leaders felt sure that the invaders were cops, and that they were seeking to plant drugs and a gun to frame the Aliens. There was also in that time some trouble with the Pagans, a rival gang. Everything was normal.

It was now a week before Thanksgiving. The night before, Scotty, who was working as a bouncer at the Fillmore East, a rock concert hall on the Lower East Side, had his head opened by an irate customer who had bounced back with a couple of friends and a tire iron. But Scotty was not by himself. It just so happened that in his time of need and trouble Groover and Vinnie came by. Groover, who had just put in a season as a $12,000-a-year accountant and two years as a college English major before finding his happiness, steamed to the aid with a large wrench. "Man, we reconditioned that motherfucker's brains," he told his brothers in a slow-motion reenactment of the incident.

"We overhauled his engine, cleaned his spark plugs, tuned him up, and did a little reupholstery." "Straight business," croaked Vinnie, a huge and gravel-voiced bearded giant, who has the ten commandments dangling from one ear lobe and a swastika on his jacket. Scotty, still applying a wet towel to a two-inch gash in the back of his head, happily told how at one point a girl friend of the bouncee took a pistol from her pocketbook and fired three shots at the assembled Aliens. None hit. "It was only a teensy-weensy little-old-lady gun," said Groover, "but they can be messy. The little holes are hard to plug and you just lay there leaking."

On that Sunday morning the recitation of the fight near the Fillmore was trivial, sort of amusing small talk. The Alien Nomads, you see, were having more serious trouble. For at about the same time that Groover, Vinnie, and Scotty were doing righteous battle with the bouncee and his band of bad cats, a potentially more serious confrontation was taking shape in the glittering halls of the New York Coliseum, that showplace of commerce and industry where vegetable peelers and vibrating easy chairs are sold at a succession of trade shows. On that particular Saturday night, the peelers and the lounges were being demonstrated alongside the chromed, lacquered, and supercharged exhibits of the National Hot Rod Show. Among the crowd of several thousand were some fifteen members of the Brooklyn and Greenwich Village chapters of the Aliens, groups tied in confederation with the Third Street Nomads. Also in attendance were three busloads of Pagans, members of a motorcycle federation that has chapters all along the East Coast. The Pagans and the Aliens do not get along. About a year earlier the last Pagan outpost in the city, a clubhouse in the East Village, was destroyed by fire, and there are some who think the Aliens may have had something to do with that. Shortly thereafter Sunshine, a former Alien, was found tortured and burned to death in a vacant apartment. Two Pagans were arrested for the crime.

The basic origin of the feud is obscure. According to the Nomads, it all has to do with that chivalrous code of honor. The Pagans, they contend, are not selective in their recruiting. They pervert the ideal and corrupt the institution. Most of their members, the Nomads say, do not live together. If one of them leaves his motorcycle at the home of another, he can't be sure of getting it back with all its parts. Other observers of gang culture say the friction has to do with the territorial imperative and is more akin to the feelings that separate the Celts and Sassenachs, the Serbs and Croats, the Profacis and the Gallos. They point out that in the geopolitics of outlaw gangs the Angels are the unchallengeable kingpins of the West Coast, in Middle America there are groups united in the Outlaws, and in point of view of numbers the Pagans seem to hold the franchise on the East Coast. Thus the Pagans see the Aliens, particularly with their ties to the Angels, as a territorial threat. And it was obvious at Nomad headquarters that the fighting that broke out at the Coliseum was regarded as serious business. It was like Kennedy finding out that the Russians were sending missiles to Cuba.

Sandy, whose time with the Marines had been spent with a crack counterinsurgency unit, set about learning what had happened. All the police could tell reporters was that as a number of Aliens stepped off an escalator, they were attacked by a number of Pagans swinging boards and sticks. Six Pagans and one Alien were arrested. Sandy questioned the Aliens who were there, and what he learned was that the Pagans had come in chartered buses and that they were after Alien patches. Each club member has two such patches, which he regards with all the reverence an Indian fighter had for his scalp. The more important is a large insignia showing a skull and the name "Aliens." This is called the colors and is worn on the back of a denim vest. The other patch is a small rectangle worn over the heart that says "1%." This refers to a statement made several years ago by the American Motorcycle Association to the effect that 99 percent of all motorcyclists are law-abiding and responsible. The Aliens say the Pagans would like to steal their patches. They would also like to take the Pagans' patches. Neal, a member of the Greenwich Village group, had his eye blackened and his patch taken at the Coliseum. He was greatly pained and humiliated by the experience and was close to tears when he talked about it.

At 2:30 on Sunday morning the Nomads, whose fifteen members represent the Alien shock troops in the New York area, began organizing. First off, Oats and Loser, who were free on bail on what they said was a "bullshit kidnapping charge," were sent away so their freedom would not be endangered. Then a lawyer who is retained by the group was called and told of the arrest of the single Alien, Paul Casey, a married carpenter from Brooklyn. He said he would be in court for the arraignment. A bondsman was also notified to stand ready. Access to the tenement was checked. Weapons were inspected and guards were posted just in case the Pagans tried to storm the stronghold. Then the various Aliens not assigned to specific tasks went off with their old ladies to their pads in the buildings to sleep. At 10:00 on Sunday morning Sandy sent a delegation of twelve to the Criminal Courts building. Their primary purpose was to be there when Casey got out, the feeling being that the Pagans might try to pick off a single Alien. A carload of club members was also sent to cruise the neighborhood of the courts looking for any suspicious comings or goings. Uncle Sal and Mario were in the courtroom. Groover, Vinnie, John-John, Maurie, Neal, and five Brooklyn Aliens stood guard in the street. Jumpin' Jac was assigned to command this group, and Sandy stayed back at the clubhouse.

For the first couple of hours nothing much happened. Vinnie and Groover entertained the assembled. "Dig it," said Groover, "you ever see two downtown diddlyboppers?" He and Vinnie began to strut toward each other with exaggerated leg and shoulder movements. "H'ya doon, man, slip me some skin," said Groover-cum-diddlybopper, extending his palm under a leg, behind his back, behind his neck to be slapped in each location in a pantomime greeting by the lumbering Vinnie. Then in a burlesque of jive talk, they had this exchange:

"How many ho you got on the street?"

"Man, I got me fifteen ho on the street."

"I got me a white Eldorado Cadillac car."

"I got *me* a white Eldorado Cadillac car."

"I got me a white-on-white shirt, a white-on-white suit, white-on-white sheets, and a white-on-white soul. Man, I am one honorary ex-nigger."

The audience laughed a lot, but one member explained that the skit should not be taken as an example of prejudice. "We ain't prejudiced against niggers, we just don't like them, that's all. Hell, we'd even take one of them into the club if we ever found any that was good enough."

The prattle and kidding lasted until about noon, when the group considered what action to take if any Pagans were to show up. They passed around a Vicks inhaler, and then five of them drifted off, returning within ten minutes. Vinnie, who had a patch saying "road runner" sewn on the crotch of his dungarees, ambled back carrying a baseball bat over his shoulder. The others who went with him had bricks, bottles, broomsticks, and staves. The courthouse is in the middle of a totally unpopulated area, and on a Sunday it is about as desolate a place as there is in New York. This was pointed out to Vinnie, who was complimented on the ease with which he found the armaments. "Well," he growled, "you know, necessity is the motherfucker of invention."

And then, as they kidded, they spotted a car with Jersey plates that pulled up to the courthouse parking lot. Four young men with close-cropped hair, neat black leather jackets, and denim trousers got out. "Look at the weekend warriors," shouted one of the Aliens as the four approached without saying anything. A single policeman stood by. The Aliens raised their taunts but, eyeing the policeman, they dropped the weapons behind a hedge. "Who's number one?" they yelled. "Nice idea fighting in the Coliseum, where do you want to hold the next one, in a police station?" The four presumed Pagans silently entered the courthouse. "Look at the schoolteachers with their hair all nice and everything. Did you bring your mother to court? Oh, Judge, I am a good boy, hardworking and everything and a family man. You let me go and I promise I'll never ride a motorcycle again," they mocked.

Less than a half hour later, the four men came out of the building after learning what was happening in the courtroom. They were followed to their car by the taunting, bat-swinging Aliens. "Who's number one?" "You all come back, you hear, and bring some friends." As the four pulled out of the parking lot, the carload of Aliens pulled out after them. A block away, the Pagans stopped for a light, and the Alien sentries on foot ran up to the car. In a stage whisper, the Pagan driver asked one of his passengers, "Hey, you got that piece ready?" But the light changed and the car sped off before any answer or any piece came. "That's the difference between them bullshit Pagans and us. Those cats are just not together. They're going to let their guys sit in jail. Shit, it's easier to find six more guys for new members than put up the bail. All they know is quantity, they don't know shit about quality." And Groover asked, "Did you hear all that bullshit about a piece? What did he think I was going to do, fall down dead? Throw up my hands like this and say, 'Ooh, you got a piece, I give up, come and get me'?" Everybody laughed and Jumpin' Jac called the clubhouse to say the car had left and was being followed.

Within a short time the Alien car returned, and its driver said he had escorted the other auto right up to the Lincoln Tunnel. Now part of the group stayed behind at the courthouse to wait for Casey, but seven Aliens started back for the clubhouse in the car, which Neal drove with screeching tires and a lot of swerving. As he swung past the right side of a cab, someone in the backseat told him to calm down. "Hey, man, cut out all this bullshit. I'm holding, so just take things nice and easy." The ebullient Groover, who extemporizes on any theme, took off in a verbal riff on this one. "Look, asshole," he told Neal, who had already slowed down, "listen good. If I am ever in a car that is in an accident, the motherfucker who's driving better pray that he comes out dead, because if he doesn't then I'm going to kill him. I hate these fucking cages and I am not about to die in one and that's 100 percent straight. The only way to die that makes sense is on your wheels or fighting with your brothers."

When the details of the court action were given to Sandy, he locked himself in with Uncle Sal and Jumpin' Jac to discuss strategy. The rest of the group sat down with five girls in the common room, which had a television set, a tape deck, and a set of rotating red, green, and yellow lights. All the appliances were on. Unlike the men, who are proud of their wild appearance, the girls were very attractive. Long straight hair in Bennington style. Very feminine, very nice. Some were mommas, the collective property of the club. They are distinct from old ladies, who live in monogamistic relationships with individual club members. Whatever their category, the girls work as waitresses, clerks, models, and cabaret folk singers. In the house they do the cooking and shopping on a communal basis. There were also some people in the house who were just friends of the Aliens. Like Charle, an attractive blonde, whose mother had come down the day before from upstate New York with a huge turkey dinner for the gang, whose members she calls "her boys." "Your old lady is out of sight," said one of the girls. "Your mother, I mean," she elaborated. "Yeah, she's out of sight, all right," said Charle.

The band of renegades also thinks highly of Momma Groover. She is a distinguished lady who lives in a well-to-do Connecticut town, and she admits to having been shocked when her son joined the group. But he and his "brothers" have visited her, and she says they have always conducted themselves "like perfect gentlemen." Privately she hopes that the day will come when Groover will leave and settle down, but she knows too, she says, that until he found his place with the Aliens he was a lost, a terribly confused young man. Groover concurs. "Until I got to my brothers it was like putting down the highway, with no idea of where I was going or what I was looking for."

Extended conversation in the living room was difficult because of the tape recorder and the television set. Some more people drifted in and seats were getting scarce. So Ginzo, a short, taciturn midwesterner with grease-stained hands, face, and clothes, came in from the adjoining kitchen and in a very quiet voice said, "One, two, three, four, cunt out of here." The girls obediently left and turned their seats over to the men, who drank Cokes and watched a movie called *The Return of Monte Cristo*. One was reading Katherine Anne Porter's *Ship of Fools* and another doodled on a guitar. And one was trying to explain to a visitor what it is that makes the group live the way they do. "About the best I can tell you is to go up to Jumpin' Jac's room and see his poem." Upstairs in the apartment that Jac shares with his old lady and their infant daughter, painted on the wall above the bed, is the poem he wrote called "Two Wheels Under Me." He said I could copy it if I wouldn't mock it. There is nothing to mock. This is how it goes:

> This is the story of a guy
>   who didn't have much in life to like
> All he had was what he wanted
>   his old lady and his bike
> When something bugged him
>   or made him mad
> He would grab his handlebars
>   in his hand
>
> The hum of his engine and
>   the wind through his hair
> He would ride down the highway
>   to his brothers who waited there
> He would look at the sights that were free
>   and say to himself this is the life
>   Two wheels under me
>
> But his girl started to tell him
>   day after day
> Honey, I love you but hear what I say
> Why don't you cut your hair and

change your style
Get off your bike and don't
be so wild
Let people talk, you would say
and let them stare
They're not in my world
so I don't care

Why can't you understand, why
can't you see
That happiness is more with
Two wheels under me

One day he was riding by
and he saw his girl
With another guy
He stopped his bike when
she called his name
She said listen—
let me explain
I wanted to love you
But that could never be
I wanted more out of life
Than two wheels under me

He said listen girl
and listen well
Remember these words I'm about
to tell
You like a person for what he is
and that's what you take
If you ask him to change
Then it's not really him
you just have a fake.
With his final word his engine roared

and with a four foot wheelie, down
the highway he soared.
Maybe to happiness, maybe to misery
But I know my two wheels will stay
under me.

Back to the events of the day. The strategy session had broken up and Sandy came down, plainly annoyed. What was annoying Sandy was the growing realization that though all he and his group really wanted to do was live communally and ride their bikes, they were being prevented from doing this by harassment from all quarters. The police, he felt, use them as a scapegoat for everything that happens; and the Pagans, with their attack, were forcing an issue. "Look, if you got the name, you got to play the game, and these jerk-offs don't really know where it's at. But if they come to New York and make trouble, everybody is going to lump us together with them. What we've got to do is to protect our home. New York is where we live, and you've got to keep your home clean."

In line with that, he has tightened discipline since taking over the presidency. "No chick gets in the door unless she's got papers showing she's over seventeen." There was a time, he said, before he was president, "when some jerk-offs would bring chicks down here and put them through their changes." But now all that is over. There are parties, of course, and women do come down. Some of them want to ball, and they do, but, says Sandy, no one is raped. "Look, man, I can't afford it." Another thing is drugs. No one is allowed to shoot dope, although there is no prohibition against softer drugs. "Discipline, that's the key. In our own way, we are very disciplined."

So, beset by all these nagging problems, Sandy moved on two fronts to protect his way of life. One was to pursue the possibility of becoming full-fledged members of the Hell's Angels. With that kind of prestige, the group would really rise above the petty squabbling they were being forced into. The second approach was to launch a public relations campaign to convince the straights in New York that, despite their hostile appearance, the Nomads were not interested in menacing the citizens and that it was in the interest of everybody's freedom that the bikers not be harassed. He went on television and talked to reporters. He stressed the group's patriotism and its acceptance of responsibility for its acts. It was a difficult position to put forward because, while he had to convince the straights of the group's basic decency and honesty, he had to avoid giving the impression to the Pagans and others that his people were turning chicken. He emphasized that his people were every one of them fighters and that they would continue to fight for the right to live together the way they wanted to, and at the same time he made the point that the Aliens were still entitled to the same civil rights as everyone else. The policy bore fruit a month after the Coliseum battle when a massive two-day party was thrown at a discotheque by the Aliens to celebrate their becoming Hell's Angels.

There have been other parties since then, thrown, says Sandy, as "gifts to our generation." The Grateful Dead played a benefit for the Angels that came off with hand-clapping joy and no violence. But in between these public appearances, which Sandy hoped would project his people in a new and positive light, the hassles on East Third Street continued. Arrests at and near the clubhouse were frequent, usually on weapons charges. There are some youth workers who have said privately that they felt the Angels were victimizing girl runaways, putting them through their changes and making them into mommas.

Sandy says such charges are ridiculous, and no woman has to stay with the Angels unless she wants to. Some people on the block say, again privately because of fear, that they are terrorized by the Angels. They say sometimes some of them come out on the street with bullwhips, scaring passersby. Police on patrol in the precinct are of a divided opinion. Some feel the presence of the Angels has contributed to the safety of the block, others that the band itself is a far greater menace to the public safety than anything it might possibly deter.

The gang itself has undergone some change, gaining a few new members and losing Groover, who, about eight months after the Aliens officially became Angels, achieved his death wish fighting with his brothers at the fourth annual Motorcycle Custom and Trade Show on the south side of Cleveland. Groover had been with a group of Angels who were attacked at the show by a larger group from the Akron chapter of Breed. Guns were fired and knives were used. The fight lasted just minutes, but when it was over there were five dead, Groover and four of the Breed. Twenty-three people were injured. Fifty-seven people, members of both gangs, were charged with murder. Groover's body was returned home. Angels came from all over the country for the funeral, paying their respects at the Provenzano Funeral Home, where Groover lay with two bottles of whiskey in his casket and his beloved Harley parked next to it. Said Sandy, "When one of our brothers dies, he doesn't really die. He stays here with us. We fight for what we believe in until the day we die and then we live on."

Witches, Wizards, and True Believers

Every weekday morning the Brentwood station of the Long Island Rail Road, like every other stop along the line, is filled with attaché case toters who are part of the great swarm that descends on the offices of midtown only to recede with nightfall to a world of shrubs and screen windows. There among the Brentwood contingent stands Raymond Buckland, perhaps a little shorter than most, but dressed as they are and comporting himself like the rest, grumbling at the delay. Reading the paper, shifting his weight from foot to foot. He has left his home on Timberline Drive and driven to the station in a hearse. The vehicle is a bit bizarre, but it was economics that dictated its choice. One needs two cars in Brentwood, and Raymond heard you could pick up a used hearse, one that had not been driven to death, or rather one that had, but slowly and with maintenance, for about $400.

This morning, as on others, he had kissed his wife and his two young sons good-bye, and he was heading for the

office of a large airline where he works. Later that evening
the trek was reversed. Again there were kisses and pats on
the head. Supper was eaten. The day's events were dis-
cussed. The children went to bed, and Mr. Buckland read
a book while his wife mended the children's socks. Then at
about ten some cars drove up to the modest green and
white cottage. Eleven men and women came to call, and
Raymond greeted his friends warmly as a bright moon
shone down on suburbia. The Bucklands led their friends
downstairs to the cellar, where everyone took off their
clothes and went into a room where a circle had been carefully chalked on a worn oriental rug. They gathered inside
it while Mrs. Buckland, a tall, slender, and attractive
woman, took her position near a dais of sorts. She wore
only a silver crescent around her neck and a silver bracelet
on her wrist. Incense, the same kind that is purchased by
the Catholic churches, was burning and sending off wisps
of sweet smoke.

It was an esbat, and the Bucklands and their friends
were practicing their religion. They are witches. Not the
kind of witches that ride broomsticks and have black cats
and stir caldrons, but the spiritual descendants of the pre-
Christian worshipers who venerated the Horned God and
the Earth Mother, adherents of a body of lore that has
been codified and kept alive through centuries of persecution. Those other witches, the ones with pointed hats and
frog's-tongue brews, never existed anyhow, says Mr. Buckland. All that was propaganda put out by the Christian
churches to drive the craft underground. "Actually," he
says in his soft English accent, "the craft is a very beautiful, very natural religion that has been much maligned. We
don't kiss the buttocks of goats or hold black masses or
worship the devil. We don't even have a devil, since that,
too, is an invention of Christianity. What we hold to are

the old ways that developed and grew as man himself developed from Paleolithic times.

"Take the business of flying. Like most propaganda, it is the distortion of truth. During some of our agricultural festivals, the believers would gather in the fields with pitchforks and would make prodigious leaps to show the wheat how high to grow. That is a very simple and quite human application of sympathetic magic. But during the centuries that it took for Christianity to overcome the old ways in Europe, some of their priests took that simple idea and turned it into the silliness about flying." There is an anthropologist at Columbia named Michael J. Harner who has studied witchcraft all over the world, and he believes that the flying business has to do with the use of psychedelic drugs used to bring the practitioner into contact with the spirit world. Belladonna, he says, may have been used as a salve by the European covens, and it often induces the sensation of flying. Mr. Buckland, who has a degree in anthropology from King's College, England, says his group never uses drugs and that he doesn't believe that the early covens did either. "Like voodoo," he says, "the craft depends mostly on rhythm as the transporting agent."

At any rate, the coven that meets in the basement of the Bucklands' house does not fly. Essentially the services are spent in devotions to the Goddess, an embodiment personifying fertility and creation. Then, too, through the combined concentrations of the thoughts and wishes of the coven members, certain magic is attempted and, according to Mr. Buckland, performed. The ceremonies vary with different times of the year, as spelled out in the *Book of Shadows*, the volume ostensibly passed down through generations, that contains the precepts of the craft. Like the ceremonies, the hand-written book, copied by the priestess whenever a new coven is formed, can be seen only by initiates. When the Brentwood coven grew large enough for members to break away and start other units, its book was laboriously copied. Today, says Mr. Buckland, the copies are used by covens in New Jersey, Washington, D.C., Baltimore, and Kentucky.

The most important days of the witch calendar are the so-called Greater Main Festivals—Halloween, February Even or Candlemas, May Eve or Beltane, and August Eve. The Bucklands keep their children home from school on Halloween, and their absence is excused for religious observance. In addition there are esbats, which occur on nights of the full moon. It says in the nonclassified part of the *Book of Shadows*, "Once a month, and better it be when the moon is full, gather in some secret place and adore Me who am Queen of all the witcheries."

The secrecy that surrounds the practices stems from the time that witches were being hunted down by the defenders of the true Church. In 1484 Pope Innocent VIII issued the bull against witches, and two years later two German monks produced what Mr. Buckland calls an "incredible concoction of anti-witchery." This was the *Malleus Maleficarum*, which gave specific instructions for the persecution of witches. All in all, Mr. Buckland estimates that nine million people were burned, hung, or tortured to death on charges of witchcraft. In the United States things are better and witches can more or less do what they like, if they do not make much noise. Some of the old stigma lingers, as when schoolchildren are taught about the Salem witch trials. They are told that of course the poor innocents were not witches, as if it would have been perfectly all right to kill them if they were. And while no one has stoned a witch for a while, they haven't been invited to any interfaith luncheons either.

In light of all this, the secrecy is traditional and understandable, but Mr. Buckland is torn by it. On the one hand he would like to debunk many of the misconceptions that he feels engulf his faith; on the other he feels honor-bound to keep certain practices a secret. He will freely explain, for instance, that the organization of the religion is controlled by the coven, a single group of witches that meets regularly at a place known as the covenstead. In the case of his own group, that is the basement room. In the craft the word *witch* can be used for both male and female practitioners, and it comes from the Anglo-Saxon term *wicca,* meaning, Mr. Buckland says, "a wise one." The coven is ruled by the high priestess, who, like the Goddess, is preeminent, and by the high priest. Mrs. Buckland is the priestess, using the craft name Rowan, and her husband is the priest or magus, and his name is Robat. In size the coven may vary widely, with its membership determined by the diameter of the magic circle in which the ceremonies are conducted. Usually this is about nine feet. "One of the beautiful things about the religion," says Mr. Buckland, who was born and raised an Anglican, "is the sense of intimacy and communion. There is a real feeling of belonging that I don't think you could get just by being in a row of people in a large, cold building." During the ceremony the priestess stands outside the circle. The lunar necklace she wears symbolizes the circle of rebirth, since a belief in reincarnation is one of the tenets of the craft. Her bracelet has three marks on it, each one denoting a degree of advancement. A member must spend at least a year and a day at each level, and when the third stage is reached he or she is eligible to become a high priest or priestess.

The craft, says the magus, who wears a short, maguslike beard, is very sensual, as life and nature are sensual. The worshipers work in pairs, male and female. And as for worshiping in the nude, or skyclad, as it is termed, he says there are two good reasons. First, it is a sign of freedom and a return to the state of nature. Even more important, though, is the belief, which Mr. Buckland says witches have long held, that certain parts of the body radiate more power than others and that these emanations would be obstructed by layers of clothing. The palms of the hands, the soles of the feet, the breasts of women, armpits, and genital organs are, he says, particularly potent sources of vibrations. In support of this, he cites experiments done at Cornell University showing that yeast cells could be killed by having a person look at or point to them. Killing yeast cells is not, however, a part of the ritual.

Each witch has several tools, the most important being an athame, or black-handled double-edged knife. It is used to make the other tools, a white-handled knife and a sistrum, or rattle, that is used to throw a beat. The coven works to the accompaniment of this tempo, dancing about and shaking. "It's hard work and it takes a lot out of you," the magus said. "Actually, we get a lot of requests to do this or that thing for someone. Cures and solutions to love or money problems. We can't possibly handle all of these, so we screen them carefully and try to help those whose petitions seem the most worthwhile." Once a petition comes up for action, the coven strains, dances, and jumps, reciting certain repetitive phrases to induce concentration. The process is a collective application of the power of positive thinking, stripped bare. The origin of this aspect of the faith, Mr. Buckland says, like every other, came naturally. "Suppose you were a Paleolithic man and you were going out to hunt antelope. Well, before you went, you wanted to do something that would ensure your success. What you did was that you staged a hunt, with a number of men dressed in antelope skins. Your success in this symbolic enactment ensured the outcome of future events.

This raised your confidence that you would do well in the real thing."

All of this made good sense to a fallen Yankee baseball fan, who remembered that in the years of his orthodoxy he spent hours swinging a special magic broomstick as he listened to radio descriptions of games in St. Louis and Chicago. He had the knowledge then that if he moved the stick just right, timing its arc perfectly to coincide with Mel Allen's narration of the pitcher's delivery, and if his feet were planted absolutely correctly on specific patterns in the linoleum, then Joe DiMaggio or Charlie Keller was going to hit game-winning home runs. The power, of course, could not be abused. It had to be saved for tight ninth-inning situations. It is perhaps significant that the Yankees have been hitting far fewer game-winning home runs since the fallen fan abandoned the ritual. Perhaps it is not.

The Brentwood coven does not accept money or gifts for attempting cures. In cases where herbs are used, the beneficiary may be asked to pay for the cost of materials. What kind of good works has the coven achieved? "Well," says the magus, "just as an example, there was a woman that one of our friends told us about who had a regressive arthritic condition. Most of the time she was confined to a wheelchair and doctors told her she would never walk normally, though she could take painful steps with crutches. We worked on that case for a long time—several hours— and about a week later I saw the woman walking down the street unaided. She said she had awakened one morning, knowing she could walk. I suppose it could be coincidence, but it's just happened too often. Another time, a woman we know, a mother of eight children, developed an ovarian growth. The doctors said she would have to have an operation, but she didn't have much money and there wasn't anyone who could stay with the children while she was in the hospital. She was quite desperate. My wife, who is a skilled herbalist, took some leaves and dried flowers, sewed them into a small cloth effigy of the woman, and we worked on the case at an esbat. Again, a week later, the woman went to a doctor for a checkup and he told her the growth had simply disappeared."

Mr. Buckland came to his belief in witchcraft through what he says was a gradual academic study of mythology and occultism. At King's College he undertook studies in anthropology and did his graduate work in Celtic lore. He had already started collecting the religious and magical objects that now take up large display cases in the room adjoining the basement covenstead. In the course of his studies Mr. Buckland came upon two books that he holds responsible for bringing about his conversion from an academic pursuit to an act of faith. The first was *The Witch-Cult in Western Europe*, in which Dr. Margaret Murray, professor of Egyptology at the University of London, wrote of the organization of a European pre-Christian religion. The second volume was *Witchcraft Today*, written by Gerald Gardner in 1954, thirty-three years after Dr. Murray's work appeared. In it Gardner affirmed what Dr. Murray had said, but added that the old ways still lingered in certain areas and that he, for one, was a witch. Mr. Buckland and his wife traveled from New York to see Gardner at his home and witchcraft museum on the Isle of Man, and they were in effect given instruction in the faith and initiated as witches in a rite that neither is free to describe. But Mr. Buckland said it bears some similarity to the tradition of the Dionysian Mysteries, and that should straighten everybody out.

Gardner, a high priest, also supplied the Bucklands with the names and addresses of correspondents in the New

York area who had read his book and were interested in the craft. These people were enlisted in the first coven that met in the Queens apartment the Bucklands then rented, five small rooms on the top floor of a two-family house. The group was economically heterogeneous and in a way quite ecumenical. There were a hairdresser, two junior high school teachers, a divorced housewife, and a college instructor. There were former Protestants, Catholics, and Jews. Lady Rowan thinks it is a marvel of New York that, despite the late-night arrivals and the beat of the sistrums and the incense smells, their neighbors downstairs never once asked what was going on, although, she says, "I'm sure they must have wondered."

The Buckland boys are associate members of the coven, and they have never hidden their religion from their friends. So far, they say, they have never been taunted or ridiculed, proving, I suppose, that either the Bill of Rights is a living document or television programs like *The Munsters* and *I Dream of Jeannie* have turned potential bigots into blasé sophisticates.

One member of the present coven—a middle-aged schoolteacher who asked that his name not be used—said that, since participating in the observances of the craft, he has come to learn "what religion is all about." There is warmth, he says, "a kindred feeling that ties me to the others. They are truly friends and I share with them the thing most precious to me—myself—and every one of them reciprocates."

Mr. Buckland likes to lecture, which he does at schools and clubs. He does not proselytize as such, but he wants people to know how witchcraft developed and what meaning it has today. Sitting on the claw-legged sofa in his small living room, he tugged on his Vandyke beard and presented a short summary of the evolution of his religion.

"The first of our Gods emerged in Paleolithic times, and he was the God of hunting. Quite naturally he was represented as being horned like the animals that were hunted, and so became called Cernunnos, the Horned One. Eventually, over generations, as hunting began to share with agriculture, he came to symbolize death and what came after. The second deity was the Mother Goddess, and she came ultimately to be the most important. The early representations and effigies showed her as a female with great pendulous breasts and the stretched belly of pregnancy. Her arms, legs, and face were barely suggested. She was the Great Provider and Comforter, a Mother Nature or a Mother Earth. She would come into dominance in the spring, both because this was the mating season for animals, and then because it was the time for sowing. The Horned One took over in the late fall, as hunting again replaced agriculture."

As proof of the natural quality of some of the forms of worship, Mr. Buckland cites their appearance all over the world in widely separated cultures. The wax figures that witches punctured with pins or burned to injure enemies have their counterparts, he said, in the rituals of Haitians, Australian Aborigines, and American Indians, as well as ancient Egyptians. To prove his point, the magus led the way with obvious pride to his collection of magical artifacts. "The oldest things I have here are these little ushabti figures," he said, picking up an inch-long figurine of a prone Egyptian, which he said was made four thousand years ago. "Now, here is a lovely concept. You see, when a person died, it was believed that his existence in the next world would be pretty much the same as his life in this one. That is, if he was a weaver, he would be expected to get up and weave. His god, or whatever, would insist that he go to work. Well, when he died, 365 of these little effigies were buried with him, and the theory was that while the deceased just lay around and rested, the figurines would take turns doing a day's work for him. Later, in Roman times, the concept, like most everything else, was corrupted, and they were turning out figurines by mass production with no similarity to the dead person."

Other showcases contained crystal balls, tarot cards, herbs, and roots. There was an Australian aborigine pointing bone, which, when spun around on a hank of hair, will come to rest marking the direction of flight of a fugitive. When that course was followed by pursuers, they would invariably come upon their man dead, smitten by the power of the bone. Or at least that's the way the story goes. There were knives and sistrums and cowrie shells used for puberty rites in the Philippines. One corner of the room was filled with a large case in which there stood a resplendent ermine-trimmed cape along with several polished and ornately engraved swords. Next to this lay a sheaf of extremely complicated diagrams. These shelves were labeled "Ceremonial Magic," and when the magus came to them he smiled and said, "Now, here's something I wouldn't want to mess with. It's just too much bother. Too much time, too much money, and too much danger. Essentially, it's not a religious operation but one in which the magician seeks to call up evil spirits and have them do his bidding. One problem is that to be successful you must obtain certain paraphernalia and it must conform to rather confining specifications. Your gown must be of purest linen woven by a virgin." Mr. Buckland grinned, adding, "That is very hard to come by these days." The shoes, he explained, must be made from the hide of an unborn lamb. Should the practitioner somehow obtain all these accouterments, he must draw three exactly concentric circles. They have to be perfect. Should even one be a fraction of a degree off, the whole thing won't work. Outside the largest circle a triangle is drawn, and a censer is placed in that space. Then you go into the middle circle and repeat some incantations over and over, appealing to this or that diabolic specter to materialize. Mr. Buckland has never done this sort of thing and doesn't know anyone who has, but from his reading he gathers that if you are lucky the smoke from the censer begins to thicken and take on the shape of some real nastiness. At that point the magician tries to coax the demon into whatever he wants him to do. It is at this juncture that danger lurks. It seems that the literature cites many examples where demons dematerialized but still hung around waiting for the magician to leave the protection of his circles and then snared him. The careful demonologist will take precautions. He might throw a live chicken out to see how it fares, or he may call for a replaceable assistant to come into the room, all the while protecting himself with amulets and clever sayings. "You see, it's very difficult. And it's not my cup of tea," says the magus who works for an airline and rides the Long Island Rail Road.

New York's occult subdivisions thrive in independent clusters. Unlike the larger and more conventional churches, they do not have public relations departments. New developments are conveyed largely by word of mouth. Each group keeps mostly to itself, although there are many who hop about the world of the occult, putting in some time with Subud and then going on to astrology, or yoga. The closest thing to an occultists' center is Weiser's Book Shop on lower Broadway, where well-dressed matrons and hippies browse shoulder to shoulder through tomes that range from alchemy to Zoroastrianism. The diversity of the paths to fulfillment is evidenced in the array, as is also the difficulty of drawing set limits to kookiness. In the front of the store are the heavies, works by Camus, Buber, Heidegger—universally accepted thinkers. Then in rapid order, stretching back, are important books on oriental religions, Egyptology, psychology, parapsychology, folk medicine, hypnotism, acupuncture, astrology, palmistry, magic, witchcraft, candle burning, ending up at the back with unidentified flying objects. Samuel Weiser founded the store thirty years ago, with no particular interest in the occult other than to make money. Today it is run by his bearded son Donald, who lives on Long Island, goes to synagogue on the high holy days, and has a very open mind toward the stuff he deals in. "People now have more leisure than ever. They are no longer satisfied with having someone else's revelations spelled out for them. What is a mystic, anyway? It's someone who talks to God. Isaiah and Augustine, they were able to communicate with God from within, and that's the underlying factor in all the occult and mystical practices, to work from within. The question is how do we get within ourselves, and it seems to me that people are trying many different ways now that they have the time and freedom. Few are going to succeed, but at least they're trying."

Of those trying, there is, for instance, Linda Patrie, a twenty-one-year-old theatrical designer. She believes completely in astrology and would not think of changing jobs or apartments or any other big move without consulting her astrologer. She has dabbled in palmistry and has felt at times that she possessed second sight. She weighs her occult beliefs against the rigid formalism of the years she spent at a Catholic convent school. "I think that in the so-called organized religions dogma has stamped out mysticism. And to me it is the mystical that is beautiful. For me the occult has so much more opportunity for delving into the self." She didn't say so, but you could tell that she also thought it was better theater. She offered another clue to the growing popularity of, say, astrology among the young—that is its scientific symbolism and language. "Science," she said, "led us away from God, and now science will bring us back."

For Henry Weingarten, a twenty-four-year-old former math major at New York University, astrology is a science. In his teakwood paneled office, illuminated by sculptured lights and outfitted with electric typewriters, Mr. Weingarten discusses wildly complicated systems of astral prediction and draws charts that range in price and detail from $6 to $110. With the persuasiveness of his own belief registering in his voice, the young man says that human existence is defined by three forces, "environment, the genetic code, and astrological force." What he would like to see is some kind of regulation that would certify legitimate astrologers and drive out the fakers, such as the gypsies, who he says cannot even draw a chart.

Among the older, steady Weiser customers is J. Hilary Herchelroth, who is listed in the classified telephone directory under the heading "Metaphysicians." A call to the number listed brings a secretary's businesslike greeting. "Oracle," she says, setting the mind to spinning images of a man in ermined vestments and a star-bedizened miter, perhaps hovering over cabalistic works. But, things being seldom what they seem, Mr. Herchelroth turns out to be no more bizarre than the average Shriner. Oracle, it turns out, is the name of his company, which produces delicious smells in a small factory in Queens. Specifically it manufactures essential oils for various cosmetic companies and scents that make stationery smell like strawberries. There is an inscription on the one-story brick building that says

"1960 B.C." This adds to the air of mystery, but Mr. Herchelroth doesn't know what it signifies. It was there when he bought the building, and his guess is that, in a momentary lapse, a stonemason got his B.C.s and A.D.s confused. The front of the place is cluttered with boxes and bottles, and everywhere there is a clash of smells, blending attars with piny aromas. From the back of the laboratory comes a large man in his sixties, dressed in farmer's overalls. He lumbers forward with his hand held out and with a crinkly smile that creases his hospitable blue eyes. "Herkleroth," he says. "The *ch* is a *k*, it's Pennsylvania Dutch." The fanciful Merlin of the mind gives way to a conventional metaphysician who makes scents.

Yes, he says, he is a metaphysician, rightly entitled to the name, having studied for a degree at the American School of Metaphysics. This, he explained, is a correspondence school affiliated with the First Church of Religious Science, of which he is an active and proud member. He lists himself in the phone book partly as a joke, but partly because he has heard that the telephone company wants to do away with the heading. "Metaphysics is an honored branch of philosophy, and I'd hate to see the directory knuckle down on it just because some people think it's quackery. So, every year I renew my listing."

For Mr. Herchelroth, metaphysics is not quackery; it is the abstract thought on fundamental concepts like being, causality, and so forth. He came to it through New Thought, the optimistic doctrine of his church. It was in the early thirties, shortly after Mr. Herchelroth had come to New York with his degree in chemistry from Franklin and Marshall College in Lancaster, Pennsylvania. He was working as a physical education instructor at a school preparing men for police department tests. "A friend of mine took me to a lecture by some guy who was saying that thinking and disease were one. I was a skeptic, so I went back three times trying to see where he would contradict himself. He didn't." Then, with gentleness, patience, and good humor, he went on to explain the beliefs he had amassed since that day. "There is something within you that is greater than any of us, and we can never be less than what it is, isn't that right? There is truth, and you can't go beyond truth, isn't that right? What is there beyond truth? There is also belief. If your belief coincides with the truth, everything is fine. But if your belief is in conflict with truth, then there is trouble. And since we cannot change truth to coincide with belief, the only way out of the difficulty is to change belief so that it subscribes to truth. Isn't that right?"

Mr. Herchelroth is credited as a healer by his church, but, he insists, "I have no more healing power than you do. The thing is, we both have a great deal." He quotes Alexis Carrel, the surgeon. "If it were not for the basic healing principle inherent in every living organism, life on this planet would be impossible."

The problem, then, is simply that of determining truth. How does he do it? "Well, in those instances where conflicts arise we must meditate, or pause and separate from the physical. We have five physical senses, isn't that right? Well, if we trusted solely to these senses, we would assume that the sun rises in the east and sets in the west, rotating around the earth. But it doesn't, isn't that right? For each sense there is a corresponding spiritual sense that must be consulted, and that's what I mean, separating from the physical. There is the inner sense of perception that is, of course, greater than just the physical sense of sight. You see much more than your eyes see. The physical sense of smell corresponds to the spiritual sense of intuition. How many times have people said, 'I smell trouble'? Then there's taste. It's a known fact we can only taste four things, sugar, salt, alkalis, and acid. The spiritual sense here is one of discretion. I don't have to tell you, you know the difference between right and wrong. Isn't that right? Finally there are the senses of touch and hearing, both of which relate to the spiritual sense of feeling. The feeling of a sunset or the feeling of being a father." Sometimes the responses of the physical senses are obvious. Other times what is required is extended meditation to free them.

Mr. Herchelroth always carries three Chinese coins of the I Ching. And the random casts of heads and tails get him past some sticklers. As to ethics, he believes that there is no such thing as good and evil. "Evil," he says, "is man's misconception of the good. If what we may regard as bad is part of the totality that incorporates everything, how can that be evil? Like Shakespeare said, there is nothing good or bad, but thinking makes it so." In a sense, this is put to the test by the elixirs his company has manufactured. "Let me ask you this, is it wrong for Jewish families to put mezuzahs on their doors? Is it wrong to carry rabbit's feet or to put a Saint Christopher medal in your car? I still think you ought to carry insurance, but is there any harm in it? I've got letters from people, most of them quite ignorant, thanking me for this stuff. One woman wrote that she had been dying of cancer, that four doctors had given her up for dead, and then, she said, she bathed with these oils and they cured her. Now you and I know that the oils didn't do it. But they gave her something to fix her faith on, and the curing process that Carrel talked about went to work. The real agent for her cure was her own power, but the catalyst may have been the oils."

Mr. Herchelroth smiled kindly and reached down into a drawer, presenting his visitor with a bookmark he had printed up. On one side it said LI DGTT FT ATI M, an inscription that was deciphered as "Lord, I do Give Thee Thanks for the Abundance that is Mine." "Those twelve words pretty well sum up my belief and my religion," said the metaphysician, looking for all the world like a man content with his abundance.

In a very old house in Staten Island, perched on a knoll overlooking the Arthur Kill, lives Elfrida Rivers, a thirty-eight-year-old woman who knows her way around the world of seers, soothsayers, mediums, and magicians as well as anyone in New York. The articulate expert is, first off, a practitioner of and believer in some of the occult crafts. She is also a science fiction writer, having written many books under a different name. Finally, she is a college-trained psychologist. "I am all but qualified to thrust myself onto a helpless public as a psychologist," she said laughingly, talking in the combination living-dining-play room. Beatle sounds blared loudly for her three-year-old daughter, who danced and scampered wearing nothing. "When you talk about charlatanism, that's where it is. There's more dogma in psychology and psychiatry than there is in astrology. No astrologer ever ordered a sixteen-year-old kid to take shock treatments for what later turned out to be epilepsy." Psychiatrists, she said, all start out believing, "but every astrologer I ever met began as a skeptic, beginning their studies to discredit the system. That, I think, is a healthier approach."

Miss Rivers, who wrote a weekly column on the occult for an East Village newspaper, says that what unites the various disparate branches of the field is a nonmaterial approach. Within this large grouping there are some charlatans, some proselytizers, and some pragmatists, who do not need proof why this or that system works but are content to know that it does. She says she is one of the latter. Grabbing hold of her mercurial daughter, she smiled and said, "I try to bring up my three children in the belief that this life is not an ultimate reality." As to the particular discipline of this or that occult practice, Miss Rivers takes the somewhat unorthodox view that it really doesn't matter. "I tell my readers that it makes no difference what you call that aspect of our lives that is operative in these things; whether it's the subconscious or the astral self is of no significance. I tell them to pick a method with which they are comfortable, one which seems to work for them."

Miss Rivers knows that she is fairly clairvoyant, and on routine matters she follows her hunches. With her husband she has developed a psychic warning system. "Say we are supposed to go someplace and I see those flashing red lights, well, I'll tell him. If he gets them too, we're just not going to go." On more serious matters she will consult her mirror. What she does to unleash her feelings is to set candles in front of a mirror and stare at the flame until she induces a semihypnotic state. Her husband will then ask a series of questions. "The first time he heard it he was scared because the answers came back in a husky man's voice. Once, before we were to go on a weekend trip, Old Charlie, the voice, ordered, 'Get the brakes fixed before you go anyplace.' That time I figured what's-his-name had flipped his wig because I had just had the car in for a thorough going over. We had the brakes checked anyway, and one of the drums was cracked right down to the hub. I've kept a record of the warnings and predictions. About three-quarters of the things have come out pretty much the way they were called. One out of fifty has been disproved outright. The others were vague or have not yet come to pass. For instance, the voice said I could and would have another baby. As a matter of fact, I conceived but I suffered a miscarriage."

All of this is only vaguely connected with Miss Rivers's religious feelings. On the second story of the old stone house there is a large, almost empty room dominated by a small table serving as an altar. This room is used by the Riverses for meetings of a small secret order, the Aquarian Order of the Rostroutan. Because it is a secret order, she cannot discuss its liturgy or practices, but she sums up its purpose by saying, "Our first vow is to abstain alike from credulity and skepticism; our second is to completely give up power over any other human being. Other than that, we are devoted to the fatherhood of God, the brotherhood of man, and the motherhood of nature."

She first became interested in occult matters as a teenager, quarreling often with her stern Scots Presbyterian father. She would read of the mystics with romantic and academic interest. "All of these things I read about were more meaningful than anything I heard in church. I loved what the Theosophists said, 'There is no religion higher than truth.' " But she didn't come around to the practice of occultism until the mid fifties, when she was living in a dull small western town with her first husband. "I answered one of those ads for the Rosicrucians, mostly out of boredom and loneliness. The Rosicrucians were once quite experimental and probing, but now I guess they are something like the Masons. Still, they provided me with a good system for meditation and study." She moved to California, where "the more I saw of organized religion, the more I liked and respected occultists. Here were people without a grinding philosophy. I still accept Christ. Christ yes, Churchianity no. Religion, a real religion, should demand more of a person than his physical presence in a building."

Her order provides her with a communion of kindred seekers, a communion that is extremely meaningful and important to her. "If there is a rough time in my life, if I read and wonder about some aspect of life, then I'm not alone. Everyone in the group who is studying it with me is my brother and sister. I can go to them and they can come to me." That need for communion, she said, is one of the dangers in the occult. It will often drive the seeking and openness into the rapacious hands of spiritual con men. "I tell my readers that 90 percent of the occult is sheer fatuity, people trying to make a buck. And trying to make profit from some real or imagined gift is as unethical as selling indulgences or paying for masses."

Jackanapes, Janissaries, and Jades

Return with us now to the thrilling days of yesteryear when from out of the west came the stealthy tread of the slick knight Lochinvar; when dalliance was in flower and gentility was praised; when the Black Death stalked the cities of man and the pox pitted visages of maids. Come to that time when men were men or janissaries or mendicants and women were princesses or courtesans or hags living out attenuated life expectancies. Come to a tournament of the Society for Creative Anachronism: here, on a lawn bedizened with crests and banners, just the hurl of a lance from a Nike missile base, already abandoned and made obsolete by the shifts of a new and quicker history. Here gather knights and ladies, who for the nonce have shed their twentieth-century roles of neuroticism, manic depression, and wage slavery and have retreated to a fanciful world of myth and pageantry. Some two hundred of them, almost all from the city, are there decked out in regalia that ranges from the rather simple bedsheet worn by Sean, the rightful Heir of Ulster, to the resplendent silks of some of the ladies and the chain-mail and lambswool armor painstakingly wrought by the Janissaries of the Khan.

They have all assembled at a trimonthly crown match at which a new king will be elected in combat. Colorful tents have been set up around the fighting ground. Small children move through the clustered multitude, selling amulets said to ward off lepers and mendicants. Seated in the shade of the largest and most ornate tent are their reigning majesties, Bruce of Newrock and his queen, Florence. On this day Bruce's title lapses. He has ruled absolutely over the kingdom for three months, ever since the day when, in the view of two very surprised New York City policemen, he dispatched the last of many pretenders in a sword fight at a Staten Island park. He presides at a competition where his successor will be chosen. Under the laws of the society, he may not defend his right to the throne. The society runs on a sort of democratic absolutism: might makes right, but only for three months at a time.

Since power, then, ebbs and flows with the fortunes of combat, a reserve of administrative authority is necessary if things are to get done, newsletters to go out on time, embroidery classes to be scheduled. For that reason, a reserve of administrative authority is vested in the seneschal, the minister to the royal household, who in medieval times was responsible for ceremonial matters. In the case of the anachronists, the seneschal is Mrs. Marion Breen, a middle-aged, robust, and hearty writer of fantasy, who with her husband advanced the society's work on the East Coast after aiding in its original formation in Berkeley. "There were a number of us out there who were interested in medieval matters, either as historians or hobbyists," says the woman whose face and bearing are simultaneously those of Anne of Cleves and Willa Cather. "One day in 1966 we all gathered in very strange costumes for a party. That was before the hippies latched onto beauty and gentleness. Everyone was protesting something or other and we thought we'd hold our own demonstration, so we marched to protest the ugliness of the twentieth century."

Unknowingly they had stumbled on an issue of fairly universal appeal, and the society grew, gaining form, definition, and a newsletter called *The Pennoncel.* When Mrs. Breen and her husband, Walter, a numismatic expert and a consultant to coin collectors, moved east, they came as emissaries of the kingdom. What with east being east and west, west, it was quite predictable that a schism would develop, and today the East Coast Anachronists are more or less autocephalic, paying no obeisance and little regard to their western progenitors, whom they scorn as nonserious dilettantes. In New York the first converts were science fiction writers such as Lester del Rey, one of the hosts for the pageant near the Nike base. Dressed in tights and a tunic, Mr. del Rey had a place of honor on the reception line that passed before the king and queen to touch off the events of the tournament. He introduced himself to their majesties as Lester the Oppressor and presented his wife as Lady Raquel the Oppressed. In addition to the fantasy people, another core of early initiates came from spelunking societies. For some reason there is an overlap of interests and outlooks among the sci-fi's, cave explorers, and medievalists. Perhaps it has something to do with getting away from it all. At any rate, from these two seedbeds the anachronists grew, gaining catholic representation. On the day of the tournament, participants ranged in age from fourteen to sixty-five. There were plumbers and factory workers as well as schoolteachers and writers. There were five blacks.

There are no rigorous requirements for membership and no initiation fees. The only strict rule is that anyone coming to a revel or pageant must be attired in some sort of medieval costume. But even here there seemed to be a good deal of latitude, since Arthur W. Saha, an engineer and chemist, walked among the caped and cowled wearing a Navajo blanket and an Indian headdress. "It's medieval," said the forty-eight-year-old Saha a bit defensively. "It's not European medieval, but it's medieval." He went on to explain that, as a Minnesota-born Finn, he was appearing as Kalavatha, an amalgam of *Kalevala* and *Hiawatha*, *Kalevala* being the Finnish national epic, a poem whose distinctive meter was cribbed by Longfellow.

As the milling and introductions continued, the revelers kept arriving at the home of Harold Dean, a Unitarian minister. He had not been a member of the society, but had turned over his house and lawns to the group after a local school board in the area had reneged on its promise to let the anachronists stage their tournament on a high school athletic field. "Those jackanapes and charlatans on the board pulled back after they learned we would have fighting and archery," explained James Randi, a writer, magician, and talk show host who appears professionally as the Amazing Randi. "What they are opposed to, apparently, is fun, and they are not alone in that opposition. It's okay for high school kids to go flailing away at each other in a football game, because that's American; but when you dress up in costumes and armor and swing sticks at each other, that's weird and suspect and probably communistic. When they first offered us the field, the school board elders must have thought that we'd just get dressed up like drag queens and stand around. I guess that would have been okay with them, provided, of course, that no one had a good time."

The opening procession ended and small groups of costumed participants retreated to sit with friends around the tree-shaded glen. Adrienne Martine, a secretary in a publishing firm, sat sewing the hem of a damask gown she had made. Miss Martine was the first reigning queen of the East Kingdom. As such, she is accorded rank and is addressed by her fellow anachronists as Prima Regina Emerita. Her consort, Elliot Shorter, a six-foot-five former military policeman, who takes the society's activities extremely seriously, is usually around to enforce this protocol. Miss Martine is perhaps slightly less serious. "If someone had a time machine and offered to transport me back to the sixteenth century, which, I suppose, is my favorite epoch, I'd say, 'Sure,' " she explained. "But first I'd say, 'Give me a week so I can get my plague shot,' and I'd probably take along some indoor plumbing devices." Miss Martine says she likes anachronists mostly because they have fun. But, she says, her involvement has been educational as well as amusing. "I've actually learned a good many survival techniques. There are women who never knew how to sew until they had to make their costumes. We also have a women's self-defense class where we study fencing, kendo, and other martial arts. I live in midtown Manhattan, and I'll tell you, I feel a lot more confident coming home at night since I started learning. We also have a dance master who teaches the gavotte and galliard, which are graceful and fun." Miss Martine unpacked a picnic lunch of twentieth-century comestibles. "You know," she said, "it's really very nice and relaxing to transport ourselves every so often to that gentler time." And with that she moved a bit to get a better view of two padded and helmeted men who had taken up three-and-a-half-foot wooden swords for the first of a series of elimination matches for the crown.

The fighters were introduced by the earl marshal, a

twenty-seven-year-old bookstore clerk. Turning to King Bruce, who was in the waning hours of his glory, the earl, who is also known as Fred Phillips, shouted, "My liege, for your amusement, may I present upon the field of mortal combat Theodore of Emerald and MacGregor of Gotz-Karlsberg." The earl marshal said a lot of other things, too, absolutely straight-faced but obviously enjoying his role. For some reason he saw fit to inform the assembled of his own lineage and title. He was, he said, "Frederic the first Earl Marshal Phillips; Grand Commander of the Loyal, Ancient, Most Noble and Honorable Order of Mount Taradhras; Warden of the Northern Marches; Keeper of Feoldwyn; Prince of Kazan; Colonel Commanding the Queen's Own LXIX Loch Sheldrake Fusiliers; Communicant of the Most Exalted Order of the Sons of the Egg; Canon Father and Professor of Ithulhuthian Eschatology." Then, with apparent reluctance to give up the spotlight, the earl gave the order to begin fighting. *"Laissez-aller, laissez-aller, laissez-aller!"* he shouted.

The fighters circled each other slowly in their bulky protective garments. Theodore attacked first with a hard overhead smash that would have dented his opponent's metal helmet had not the MacGregor parried. "Oh, well put and well defended!" shouted the earl marshal, thankful for the opportunity to say something. In a series of swift banana steps, the MacGregor moved swiftly toward the slower, though heavier, Theodore. MacGregor flails and knocks the wooden sword from Theodore's grasp. Then, rather than pressing his advantage, he steps back to allow Theodore to retrieve his weapon. "Oh, quite chivalrous, very chivalrous!" shouts the bouncy earl marshal, and the crowd applauds. The fighters become cautious. The kilted MacGregor dodges in and out, and for nearly a minute no blow is struck. "What have we here, a couple of bindle

stiffs?" some shout. But then, as if in response to such derision, MacGregor becomes an offensive dynamo. He
swings his weapon like a lasso, thrusting here and batting
there in a two-handed motion. There is a thwack!—the
definite sound of contact—and the fight is interrupted mo-
mentarily so that the earl and Mr. Shorter, the former military policeman who is acting as the Juge de la Geste, can
deliberate. They agree the blow was fairly struck and that
it would have rendered Theodore's left arm useless. Consequently he is ordered to throw away his shield and fight
on. Now the Highlander presses on without mercy. He
whips down in a long arc, catching the tiring Theodore on
his padded jerkin just over the left clavicle. Again the fight
is stopped, and the large Mr. Shorter announces, "The
blow is judged to have sufficient force to have cloven a
quarter of an inch of Maximilian armor." Hearing this,
Theodore falls to the ground dead and, in accordance with
the bylaws of the society, remains so for a full ten seconds
for the convenience of photographers.

Theodore the Emerald, who is really Theodore Greenstone, a twenty-eight-year-old advertising salesman, re-
moves his padding and congratulates MacGregor of Gotz-
Karlsberg, who is really Joseph Russell MacGregor Seitz,
a twenty-one-year-old special student at M.I.T. who takes
fighting seriously, having been a consultant to both the
Army Limited Warfare Laboratory in Aberdeen, Maryland, and the late Biafran government. In Biafra he in-
structed the troops on the synthesis of chemical fertilizers
and the manufacture and use of crossbows. MacGregor
Seitz is a tall thin fellow, and his mannerisms of speech
could easily be mistaken for a put-on; on first hearing him,
it's easy to mark him as a phony or braggart. But that's not
it. He's really talking about what he knows and what he
does, which is just a lot different from what most other

people know and do. MacGregor Seitz marches to a different oscilloscope. For instance, when he described his work with the crossbow in Africa, he noted, with only the slightest trace of humor showing, "I might add that despite several early bulls on the subject I have not been excommunicated for my work with crossbows." Two weeks after the tournament, the young scientist-historian-warrior had his picture in the newspapers of America, posing with the actual, real nuclear reactor that he had built out of tin cans and spare parts for a total cost of slightly more than $1,000. There have been no bulls on nuclear reactors.

Anyway, after his bout with Greenstone and after people had heard him talk, MacGregor of Gotz-Karlsberg became favored to walk off as the day's victor. But there were still many contenders to be dealt with, and the bouts continued with frequent intermissions for such peaceable pursuits as puppet shows, archery exhibits, and a concert given on the virginal, which, it was explained to those mired in the twentieth century, was an instrument that, despite its name, fathered the harpsichord. An acting troupe from Greenwich Village performed the final scene of *Hamlet* with remarkable swordplay. Two teen-aged brothers from Long Island, who had spent three months fashioning their intricate chain-mail janissaries' uniforms, stripped to shorts and gave an exhibition of Greco-Roman wrestling. Meanwhile the elimination bouts continued until only two pretenders remained: MacGregor and Sir Iolf Stevenson, an Icelandic noble who came with his bagpipes and kilts. Sir Iolf was secretive about his true identity, explaining that he was employed by the National Aeronautics and Space Administration as a scientist and that his project director might be less than overjoyed to learn of his backsliding into primitive technology. The fact that both regal candidates were technician-scientists was significant.

Throughout the crowd there were quite a few like these, men and women whose working lives were spent in the rational unraveling of present-day mysteries. They were distinct from and yet compatible with the large science fiction and fantasy contingent. Some people in the crowd commented about this commingling of such disparate folk, but none really fully explained it. Maybe, said the wife of the hosting minister, some of these people have hit their fact threshold and are seeking answers in fancy. Another woman suggested that those who deal in dispelling mysteries probably realize that man needs magic or questions almost as much as he needs answers, and that all the gaiety of the day, built so completely on a past that probably never was, actually stems from despair with a present that most certainly is.

By and large, though, people were not concerned with introspection but with having a good time. If the basis of the day was escape, the fugitives from time were not worried about the posse. What was of immediate concern was the crown match. On opposite corners of the fighting ground, MacGregor and Sir Iolf were being dressed in their pads and helmets by clusters of their partisans. Like the day's other combatants, the men were not just flailers and slashers but fighters who had actually trained for combat. Some worked out at their homes with teeterboards to gain balance. They spent hours squeezing rubber balls to strengthen their wrists and forearms to control their heavy weapons better. The rules of combat had become very formal during the life of the society. A fighter could, for instance, elect to discard his shield, substituting a dirk. To make such a decision, one would have to weigh the style of the opponent. If the man you were to fight was a cautious, opportunistic battler who would seek out small advantages before advancing, a shield would be necessary. If, on the other hand, he was overly aggressive, flailing away in wild rushes, you could probably evade his fury and counter with either hand, so a shield would not be so important.

While the preparations for the main event continued, Bruce of Newrock was explaining to newcomers that the only medieval hand weapon absolutely prohibited in the tournaments was a morgenstern, the spiked ball at the end of a chain. "There is no defense against it," he said. "If the chain is long enough, you can wrap it around a shield and yank it from your opponent's grasp." From where he was sitting, you could look across the lawn and through trees to a sign on the adjoining property that said "Battery D of the Nike Defense System." The sign, like the base, was overgrown with weeds.

The two fighters, now dressed for combat, were introduced to Bruce. The fighters were questioned and, as usually happens in affairs of state, problems arose. For one thing, Iolf pointed out that he was due to go on some sort of quest for NASA and, were he to win, he would not be able to officiate at the crown match three months hence. For another, MacGregor spends most of his time in Boston, and the society's sovereignty did not yet encompass that northern outpost. Then, too, neither man had a lady with him, and the laws of the society clearly stated that no man can assume kingship unless he has a queen. King Bruce consulted with the seneschal, and since everyone involved was pretty sophisticated, most of the problems posed were overcome. It was decided that, should Iolf win, he would simply appoint a regent to act in his stead. Should MacGregor be victorious, he would simply set up a temporary new seat of the kingdom on the banks of the Charles, coming to New York for whatever revels were to be held. But the question of the ladies provided opportunity for intrigue. The chief schemer was a sixteen-year-old plump high school girl from Queens named Elizabeth Portnoy, who stood on the fringe of the negotiations with some of her friends and said in a stage whisper that carried loudly, "Listen, I must be queen. I will do anything to be queen. What should I do?" The girl next to her suggested, "How about a little poison in his ear?" Another advised, "How about just asking one of them to let you be their queen." But Miss Portnoy sneered and said, "Oh, I know, I will promise to sing all of Gilbert and Sullivan to him." Her friend, a sixteen-year-old who described her costume as being that of a fifteenth-century tart, responded, "That should finish your chances completely." Miss Portnoy was not to be easily dissuaded. "You just don't understand. I must be queen. I must. I will stop at nothing." But, plot as she would, it came to naught, for both fighters admitted they had ladies available who would be happy to share the throne.

The fight could now begin. The earl marshal shouted *"Laissez-aller!"* and the swordsmen began smashing and blocking. Both men received some well-put thwacks and welt-raisers. "My God," said a spectator in monk's robes after a particularly furious exchange that left the bare legs of both fighters splotched with pink that would later turn black and blue, "smoting may be dangerous to your health." The match lasted for about ten minutes. It ended when MacGregor, who was down to the use of only his right arm, his left one having been deemed severed, took off Sir Iolf's head, or would have if the swords were not of wood. He was crowned with laurel and ascended to the throne. Everybody drank punch, tea, coffee, or beer. The sun was setting. People drifted off, still costumed, for their cars and to catch buses that would get them back to the city and to a time of less stylized slaughter. It was one hell of an election day.

To the Memory of Albert-Alberta

There is in this city an official Landmarks Preservation Commission, whose members work like the underdogs in a Monopoly game trying to save quaint old Ventnor Avenue from the rapacious real estate moguls. The commission has, by and large, done its job well, plaquing certain Victorian mansions and designating certain parts of the city as historical districts, whose alteration must conform to whatever style prevails there. But there is one area they have missed. Times Square. True, the epoch that this garish, illuminated, and bizarre plaza represents is not baffled in the kind of genteel sentiment of say, Brooklyn Heights or Waverly Place. But it is certainly the quintessential architectural and cultural paragon of the age of electricity, the 1920, 1930, and 1940 years, when hordes would come and gape at the lit-up, flashing, mobile, sexy streets, an acromegalic Wurlitzer jukebox with colored fluids streaming over and around the tiny people.

The square, particularly the block of Forty-second

Street between Seventh and Eighth avenues, is the city's own repository for the cultural aspirations of Centralia, Illinois, the land of the lumpen, where spiritual descendants of now-old American dreamers sell their blood and dream their dreams of Mercury convertibles. I know for sure that after the street is demolished to clear the way for fancy, sterile, and commercially profitable offices, someone someplace will reconstruct it like Dodge City, a museum shabbily reflecting the time in which men with waffle shoes and yellow-haired women in sequined sunglasses escaped the structure of Rotarian life, capturing the electrical essences through the range finders of their Kodaks.

The street is already a museum, the city's gaudiest anachronism. Once its rationale lay in its proximity to Grand Central Station. To come to New York meant to arrive at the terminal, to walk or ride the few blocks to the Great White Way, and there to marvel at the overwhelming extravagance of flashing lights, rooftop waterfalls, and the vapor that escaped from the mouth of the Camel Man. But now you come into the city at La Guardia or Kennedy, and Times Square is a place you avoid. Just for a few, New York begins at the Port Authority Bus Terminal, which is at Forty-first and Eighth. So what has happened is that the economic base of the street has shifted from the modest but solvent family group to the cardboard-suitcase migrant. Toffenetti's with its sit-down, strawberry short-cake crowd has given way to Nathan's, where you can eat hot dogs, hamburgers, or clams while standing up and passing through. Pizzas, knishes, and $1.79 charcoal-broiled steaks are the staples of the block. The movies are still a major attraction, but they are different movies. Skin flicks like *Wild Pussy* and *Motorcycle Gang Bang* have replaced the June Allyson–Jimmy Stewart sagas of good decent folk, in and out of sensible kinds of trouble. No longer do dating teen-agers come down from Brooklyn and the Bronx for special dates. Now they go to the East Side. The balcony of the Paramount, which pulsated with the libidinous shrieks of a pre-teenybopper time, is now an extension of the editorial offices of *The New York Times*, and there is not even a plaque to commemorate it as the place where hundreds upon hundreds of adolescent boys grappled with hooks and eyes to cop their first bare tit.

Today the block between Seventh and Eighth has, in addition to the movie houses, several army-navy stores and a blood bank, where convicts just out of jail can get ten dollars or so with which to start a new life. And there are several Fascination parlors, where, at ten cents a game, intense players, most of them men and most of them fairly young, spend hours rolling a little black ball at a board with twenty-five holes, hoping to fill out a horizontal, vertical, or diagonal line before anyone else does. If they are successful they can win coupons. If they win enough coupons they can win a transistor radio or a hair dryer. With the worst sort of luck, one can lose about three dollars in an hour, but the time is spent in drama, and it is true that in every game some loser wins. There is also a penny arcade, where the new electronic games are replacing the old manual and electric ones. For a quarter a player can, for instance, man the periscope of a submarine and release zooming torpedoes at battleships streaming along a horizon. For a dime he can face down an automated bad guy in a duel. He puts his dime into a console next to a holster with a pistol that shoots some kind of electronic impulse. Some twelve feet away is an articulated mannikin dressed all in black, with a scowling, sneering face. Once the coin goes down a recorded voice drawls, "Ah'm gonna referee this h'ya shoot-out. When I say draw, you draw. Okay? Now draw." The player reaches and fires. He misses. Another voice drawls, "Ya missed me that time, ya yellow-livered dude. Why don't ya try again?" Another "draw." This time, the player gets there first. "Aaaaaargh, ya got me that time, ya dirty polecat," groans the voice. Sometimes a man will duel for more than a dollar's worth of three-shot showdowns. Hardly anybody ever goes to the strength tester or the electric foot vibrator anymore. Most people in the place are teen-aged blacks, proving possibly that ontogeny recapitulates phylogeny, but that is a heavy thought, one that I'd readily recant under the least pressure.

It is, however, the basement of the arcade that to me will always symbolize the street and what has happened to it. Outside, on the street level, the sign still says "Hubert's Flea Circus and Museum—See Live Acts." That's the basement, but there haven't been any live acts since 1965. Still, for the same ten cents that it costs to duel with an electronic dummy, you can go down to the basement. It isn't what it used to be. Now, on the same stage where I saw Albert-Alberta, the symmetrical hermaphrodite, sits a color television set watched by four acned time killers. In an anteroom, where once a henna-haired and fat nude bounced balloons in a claw-footed and eroded bathtub, there is a musty diorama depicting the living room where the Collier brothers, scavenging millionaires, ate Spam out of cans, collected old newspapers and rags, and died in the early fifties. For the same ten cents, you could, back then, watch a comely black woman dance with a tired snake wrapped around her dancer's neck. Sometimes she would coax it into daring strikes at the spectators' heads. There was also a strong man who lifted things and an artist who gave a chalk talk, changing one 1920 hairdo into another by dabbing at it with a damp sponge. It was a hell of an act in the fifties. There was also the elephant-skin girl and the tattooed lady with a crucifixion scene on her back. "When I go home at night, my husband asks me to shimmy. That way he gets to see moving pictures," she would say.

It was hardly spectacular, but it served to warm up the audience for the big stuff that came later at a quarter a shot. First there was the truly remarkable Albert-Alberta, who delivered her tale of marvelous tribulation as she/he sat upon a small stage in a silken bathrobe, speaking in a husky, throaty voice. She began life as a happy, active farm girl in Alsace, growing to beautiful, blushing woman-hood and marriage. In her twenty-first year she gave birth to a child and shortly thereafter she underwent some changes. It seems she split right down the middle. She would loosen her bathrobe and, grabbing a right breast covered in a demi brassiere, would say, "This side represen' the feminine," and then, pointing to a somewhat smaller flab on her left side, "This side represen' the mas-culine." She would show a hairy left foot and a smaller, smoother right one. There was a five-o'clock shadow on half of her profile, and a lot of pancake makeup on the other. In answer to questions from the audience, she ex-plained that the law forbade her to demonstrate her condi-tion any more specifically, but that for an additional quar-ter she could sell a small pamphlet with pictures that would explain everything, providing all the scientific evi-dence. The pictures turned out to be line drawings that shed little light on the mystery.

Her spiel over, the audience was now herded into a side room, laying out another quarter. There it could watch the woman in the bathtub. The tub was on a platform, and from what was visible to the audience it was impossible to say what the plump lady had on, if anything. But the smarter teen-agers took their cue from the seeds and, instead of facing the tub, turned around and looked at a strategically hung mirror. If no one was in their way, they could catch a glimpse of nipple, or they thought they did, which is the same thing.

From here the group, perhaps about twenty in all, was directed into clean, cozy quarters where Professor Roy Heckler put his fleas through their stuff. He sat there impassive, behind a white piece of felt the size and shape of a checkerboard. Once the shuffling had stopped and there was a short period of dramatic silence, the professor would begin in his rumbling bass. From performance to performance, the cadence and the words never changed. Why meddle with perfection? "What you are about to see is a number of acts per-formed by hu-man fleas. They are called hu-man fleas be-cause they sub-sist en-tirely on human blood." The professor, a large man with the slightly contemptuous bearing of someone who knows he can do difficult things, then took out a test tube with a harnessed flea inside and a magnifying glass outside. "The first step in training a flea is to change its traditional manner of lo-co-motion. In its natural habitat, a flea hops up and down. But for our purposes we want him to walk straight. In order to have him do this, we place the tiny fellow in a tube like this, which we then keep on its side. When the flea hops, he hits his head on the tube and in due time he learns to walk cor-rectly." The next step, he droned on, was to harness the wee beast with a wire to train it in its specialty. At this point he would open a drawer and remove three chariots resembling bangles from a charm bracelet. From the front of each a wire led to a tiny module that might have been a superminiature nuclear reactor, but was probably a flea. The professor prodded the felt with a whip and shouted, "Go, Horatio," and, by God, Horatio would go, jerking the chariot behind him for about two inches before stopping. And then Juvenal and Orestes would also go and stop, and go again. And in a matter of seconds one of them had crossed the finish line, drawing cheers and laughter from the assembled.

With no pause for flummery, the professor moved on, bringing out a music box and the world's tiniest dance troupe. The dancing fleas were dressed in tiny cones of red and yellow, and when the music played, the cones twirled round and round. It was a magnificent performance. Finally there was Sampson, the world's strongest flea. His task was to turn a small jeweled carrousel, about two inches in diameter and weighing a couple of million times his weight. The professor likened the feat to a man's picking up the Empire State Building, I think, with his nose. Anyway, Sampson got the carrousel to twirling. He may even have taken a bow. Then he went back in his box and the show was over.

At different times there were other acts at Hubert's as well. For a while there was a large-nosed, gawky fellow who sang in falsetto as the Human Canary. He went on to fame as Tiny Tim. There were fire-eaters, sword-swallowers, and armless people who wrote with their toes. Their pictures now hang in the basement room, and Harold Smith, the manager and a former performer himself, takes pleasure in explaining their acts to anyone who asks. Mr. Smith is sixty-four years old. He wears a busboy's jacket and he keeps the downstairs room clean and acts as a curator of a recent past. In 1965 he was still doing his specialty and serving as master of ceremonies for the eight shows that went on nightly. His act, which he had also taken on the road with the Barnum & Bailey show, consisted of playing popular show tunes by rubbing the rims of champagne glasses. He had done it since he was a kid in high school in Ellenville, New York, but he didn't turn professional, he says, until he got out of the army in 1947. That's when he appeared on the Ted Mack *Amateur Hour* and then joined the circus. "I loved the traveling. We played in Mexico, Hawaii, Cuba, Canada, and all over the United States. I was with the sideshow, and I'd line up my glasses and play numbers like 'Lady of Spain,' 'Anchors Aweigh,' and 'The World is Waiting for the Sunrise.' " Mr. Smith says that as far as he knows he was the only one who could make music by rubbing glasses, although there were others who hit them with mallets. "The hardest thing about my act was keeping my hands clean and dry. When you play eight shows a day, you have to keep washing your hands and drying them constantly because the slightest bit of moisture can throw you off."

Like most of the acts, he would earn about $85 a week. Some of the bigger attractions got as much as $150, and Jack Johnson, the legendary black boxer, earned $300 back in 1939, when he did a strong man routine there. Mr. Smith, of course, was not around then. The acts he remembers best were Sylvia Porter, the girl with the largest feet in the world, who never wore shoes, an escape artist named Mangin, and Laurello, the man with the revolving head. Mr. Smith does not think it was television or changing tastes that killed the shows. "No, sir, I'm sure people would still love to see live acts, but what did them in was inflation. We would charge ten cents admission and a quarter for some of the special acts, but then the acts had to be paid more. Most of our business, believe it or not, was families with kids. If we raised prices, these people could never afford it." So right now the downstairs remains a relic where four or five kids wander in each hour not knowing exactly what to expect. They'll peer into the stereopticons where the world's largest collection of art rendered on pinheads is housed, and they'll look at the reconstructed disarray of the Collier brothers' living room.

In addition to Mr. Smith, the only other more or less permanent resident of the place is Bernard Wolfe, a somber eighty-seven-year-old gnome and show business veteran of more than fifty years. He gets to Hubert's each day during the spring, summer, and early autumn at 2:30 P.M. He sits by an electric coffee maker under a sign that says, "Your Portrait, by Bernard, $3.50." "I'll tell you the truth, I set the price high because I don't want a lot of work. One or two sketches a day is enough, I just do this to keep busy," said the red-smocked, hunched artist. "In the winter," he went on with grave seriousness, "I leave here and go to Miami, where I sit in the window of Nizener's five-and-dime and draw portraits there. Sometimes days will go by without a customer. But I don't care, I'm not in this for the money. You see, I'm a natural-born artist and I like to keep busy," he said without a trace of humor. Actually, and somewhat surprisingly, Mr. Wolfe was a natural-born comic and impresario until he was fifty years old. "I started out on the Lower East Side as a burlesque comedian, and after a couple of years as a single, I put together a show called 'Bernard Wolfe's Amateurs.' We'd go upstate and play in Schenectady and Albany and places like that. One time a fellow in the Troy paper wrote we were the best show to come into town that year—it was around 1923. I'd be the master of ceremonies and there would be singers and skits. Sometimes we used local people or we'd have amateur talent contests." His best act, he remembers, was Aunt Jemima. "She was a big Negro woman and she'd just sing one number, 'Sweet Georgia Brown.' She would sing and shake her big ass and the crowd would love it. If she's alive now, she must be ninety-five. But maybe fifteen years ago I was in Coney Island and I saw her in a show out there singing 'Sweet Georgia Brown' and shaking her ass. She was still terrific."

It was in 1930 that Mr. Wolfe determined that vaudeville was approaching a dead end and that he'd better switch to something else. "I took one look at the talkies and I knew I better get out. Well, like I said, I was a natural-born artist. I never took any lessons, but I could capture a likeness right off the bat. So I started doing sketches at the Chicago World's Fair. Then I went to a nightclub in Baltimore and to the Mexican Village in California, and I sketched pretty much all over the United States. You see, I developed this technique of doing the portraits in color. Most of the other sketchers would only use charcoal."

If Mr. Wolfe doesn't want to be too busy, the third remaining member of Hubert's entourage is restless and can't wait to get back to work. She is Estelline Pike, whose job now is to make change in a booth in the upstairs arcade and to sell admissions to the museum. The widow Pike, who is sixty-one years old, is referred to by Mr. Smith as the "world's greatest female sword-swallower." But she scoffs at the description. "How can you be the world's greatest anything unless you work at it?" But behind the modest disclaimer there is a sense of pride, and you know she knows she is the best. She is a friendly, chatty, Kansas-born show woman, who has worked in small carnivals and big circuses all over the United States. She started coming to Hubert's in 1957 during the winter layoffs, and when the circus dropped its sideshow a few years ago, she began working in the change booth. She likes to talk about the old days and particularly how she got into the sword-swallowing business. It was about 1927 and she was fresh out of the Barnes Commercial College in Denver and living in Kansas when a small carnival run by

John G. Bull came into town. John G. Bull was not only the owner, but, as Prince Lucky, its main attraction, sending rapiers and swords down his gullet. Anyway, Estelline and Prince Lucky were married and after much cajoling she finally got him to teach her the art. "At first, he wouldn't listen to me, but then I asked him what would happen if he got sick. That made the difference and he started teaching me. There are no tricks in sword-swallowing, no disappearing blade, you just have to learn to control your throat and esophagus." She learned well enough to drop four swords down her throat at once. And the finale of her show was the swallowing of a seven-and-a-half-pound cavalry sword. "I'd pass the thing around and kibitz a lot before swallowing. That's one of the secrets. You don't want to work as hard as you have to. I used thirteen swords in my act, but you want to talk a lot and you have to control the crowd. That's the secret of carnival acts. In a nightclub there's a lot of messing around. A performer can even get drunk and do all right. In a carnival, you may have a hundred people watching you. They're not there to drink or chat, just to watch you, and you have to keep their attention at all times. By the time I got to my finale I'd have complete control. I'd pass the big sword around, and they'd touch it and feel it. Then they watch me lower it, just letting it go down slowly of its own weight all the way down to the hilt. It's hard for me to see them, but I can feel their eyes. Then when it's all the way down to the hilt, twenty-seven inches down, I start bringing it up, and at the end I flip it out and catch it in midair. The whole act takes twelve or fifteen minutes, but most of it is talking. You do five or six shows a day and, I'll tell you, that's work."

Mrs. Pike has been with large shows like the Royal American, which travels in its own eighty-car train. She has been in and has run small carnivals. And she has been on television. Through it all, she raised three children, a married daughter in California, another daughter who is a professional bowler, and a son who is a sword-swallower. What Mrs. Pike misses even more than performing are the friendships of traveling shows. "You work with these people, you travel with them, and you live with them. It's like a family." The motherly sword-swallower reached into an overstuffed handbag and found a letter she had received that morning that an armless friend had typed to her with his toes. "We all try to keep in touch." This last letter contained the news that a sword-swallower named Orlando had had an accident in Mexico doing an act with a fluorescent bulb. This, she explained, was an act in which a specially made bulb is swallowed and lit. She never had any trouble with it, but there have been cases where a sudden movement can cause the glass to shatter. The only time she did have some trouble was once when a man in the audience kept taunting her, saying the act was a trick. She lost control and continued performing even after her act should have ended. "I was angry and nervous and in a sudden move I punctured my esophagus."

For the two weeks that it took her to recover, the circus folk looked after her. Those whom she felt particularly close to, she says, were the freaks. She never patronized them and she doesn't think they ever envied her. "Hell, how can you be condescending to someone who's getting $200 more a week than you are?" She remembers vividly an armless girl named JoAnn Beach who was married to a knife-thrower. "I'd go over to her trailer for a drink, and I tell you that woman ran her house better than I ran mine. She had two little girls, and she'd go about her business as we chatted, making the beds with her feet, spanking the kids if they got out of line. She could type, mix drinks, and

Michael T. Kaufman

do just about anything. There was just nothing you could
pity her for." Another she remembers was José deLeon
from Mexico, who was born without limbs, but could
paint beautifully, holding a brush in his mouth, and speak
five languages. "I remember him saying, 'I was born this
way because God wanted to make me special. He wanted
me to show people what they can do.' "

A few times a day Max Schaeffer, whose family owns
the arcade and the museum, wanders into the place. He is
in his sixties, which is old enough for him to miss the Hubert's that was. Why, a visitor asked him, did he have to
do away with the acts? "You see, you just can't get the acts
anymore. You can't find any more good freaks," he replied. And why was that? he was asked. Mr. Schaeffer
shrugged, spread his hands, and answered, "Medical science, I guess."

Billy Budd Meets the Fortune Society and Thus Saves His Soul and Ass

On a drizzly and cold autumnal night, Chuck Bergansky, who knows loneliness as other people know their mothers, was locked inside a rented Westchester room watching a television panel show. Some leggy woman with streaming hair was saying what she likes her men to smell like, and Chuck Bergansky continued doing heavy time. Then the camera's eye moved to four men seated around a table, and Holy Christ! one of them was Charles MacGregor. The same muscular Charles MacGregor who would always be laughing and stealing packs of cigarettes up at Dannemora, the prison-wise con who had been on the spot with Chuck and who was talking now about the way that prison refines and polishes the character disorders of the men who go there. As he and the other men from the Fortune Society talked, Chuck Bergansky, who had almost inured himself to isolation, was swept with yearning. That thing that started somewhere around his stomach and spread through him, that thing that in the past made him get a gun and extort respect, now coursed through his mind and body. And, as he had been doing with increasing regularity, Chuck Bergansky asked, "Who and what the hell am I?"

The answers were still forming. A bastard son. Lithe and muscular, with a broken nose. A thirty-six-year-old failed stickup man who had spent twenty-four years in confinement. A lonely son of a bitch. A man who hadn't been free for more than a year since he was sixteen. More specifically: a man who had lied his way into a job as a roofer after coming out the last time, who had hurt his back on the job, and who was getting $80 a week in compensation after an operation. A very lonely son of a bitch. He had been good since coming out. But the last couple of weeks had been worrisome. He would read in that room and watch television and take walks. He had no friends. He was feeling himself slip. He started hanging out in bars and playing in back-room card games. He'd want to meet women, but if he liked them he knew he couldn't tell them who he was and where he'd been. If he didn't like them he felt depreciated and clammy for coming at them with his need.

And there was Charles MacGregor, with his shiny shaved black head, talking all serious about speaking at colleges and working to arouse a public awareness about prisons, talking about coming to terms with yourself. MacGregor, who had pulled four hundred stickup and stomp jobs, who had done the black thing in the joint— make the jokes, slide with time, but keep out of the line of fire. Bergansky couldn't put him down. Once Bergansky had led 162 men on a prison strike, and they had beaten him and the others with sticks and he had made the hole for ninety days. Three months in a strip cell on one meal every two days, no talking, no washing, no shaving. All the strikers were white. The blacks couldn't afford rebellion. They would have been killed. But there was MacGregor now, standing up and saying things. And more importantly, there was MacGregor, with other people like himself, sharing perceptions of time and space formed in a lifetime of standing count, living by the bells, and having a number instead of a name.

The next morning Chuck Bergansky took the train to New York and came to Fortune's office. It was then a two-room office on Broadway near Forty-fifth Street, where the group's founder, David Rothenberg, was still doing business as a Broadway press agent. A couple of years ago David was making $900 a week doing publicity for Broadway shows. He is, in manner and style, very unlike a press agent. Small and gentle, with a voice that gets lost across a room. His eyes are sad. Chuck Bergansky calls him Jesus Christ. He calls Chuck Billy Budd. David has never been confined in anything more restrictive than the Ethical Culture's Encampment for Peace or his job in the ballyhoo business. The thirty-five-year-old New Yorker's first love had been theater, and he had written a few plays before economics and circumstances led him to become a press agent. But he recoiled from show business and kept dreaming of theater.

A few times he produced plays, and one was *Fortune and Men's Eyes*, by John Herbert, a Canadian who had been sent to prison as a confused sixteen-year-old. The play, set in a cell block, shows how what George Bernard Shaw called the crime of imprisonment drains humanity from all whom it touches. A few things happened while the play ran. For one, a federal agent approached Herbert, the playwright, in the lobby one night and told him that as a convicted felon he would have to go back to Canada or face deportation. His only conviction had been on a framed-up sex charge twenty years earlier, which formed the basis of the play. Herbert left, and David became enraged. The next thing that happened was that after one performance a man rose from the audience and proclaimed that the play was true, that it depicted reality as he had seen it during twenty years inside. The man returned, bringing with him other former convicts, and after each performance panel discussions were held on stage. Correction officers sometimes came to take part. It was good publicity for the play, and it seemed a clever gimmick. But the play closed.

The discussions went on. A nucleus was formed, and David started traveling to high schools and colleges with his growing entourage of former gunmen and killers. A newsletter was created and a radio program was produced, to be aired weekly on WBAI. There was a good deal of true confessions, very sexy, very bold, in the panels. Pat McGarry told of his twenty-four years of small bits strung together in joints from coast to coast. Pat, who dressed flashily and wore an earring in his ear, would tell how he was a homosexual but also a human being. He would tell of the time he slashed his wrists because a warden had promised him to a cell block as a reward for their good behavior. Clarence L. Cooper, Jr., a black novelist who had done time before and after having been published, told how he was put in solitary confinement at the federal detention center in Lexington after he had smuggled a poem out to the *Saturday Review.* After the sessions, sweet young girls and kind youths would come up and bask in the romance of talking to real bad guys.

Some of the original group left. Some went back to jail. David loaned money to men coming out, who would never be seen again. Former convicts were sleeping on his living room couch. Some took things and stole off in the night.

He was becoming wary, but Fortune continued. They were talking at colleges, widening consciousness. The warden at Rahway prison in New Jersey allowed David to talk with inmates. The New York State system, though, was hostile. The newsletter was ruled contraband and inmates were forbidden to get it. But the word spread inside, and upstate MacGregor, for instance, had heard about Fortune. At Green Haven prison, Prentice Williams, who was finishing an eleven-year term for armed robbery, heard about it and wrote to David. Prentice had not received a single letter during the first six years he was inside. He used to write for catalogs just to get something with his name on it.

Fortune, whose first mission was propaganda, was now turning its attention to welfare. Men coming out were clothed. They got reinforcement from each other through the hard times of job interviews. The parole board was more kindly disposed toward the group than the prison system. It ruled that men coming to Fortune's office would not have their parole revoked on the ground of consorting with known criminals. But Fortune was not so kindly disposed to the parole board. They kept attacking the idiocy of a release contract that determined good behavior in terms of not cohabitating with a woman after being kept away from women for long periods. This is what Fortune was when Chuck Bergansky walked in the door.

He didn't need the money or the clothes. He needed, he would say later, what he had been looking for all his life, friendship, communion, family. "I remember I came down and talked with Charlie, and then I just started hanging around. Every morning I'd take the train in from Westchester and I'd sit around the office. At night we'd go to a theater. I'd never been to the theater before, and it opened things up for me. I had always read but now I had people I could talk to about what I'd read and seen. I started working, just typing, going to the post office. Stuff like that." Chuck is extremely energetic. He moves like the white hope of the Comstock Reformatory that he once was. His speech is a parody of the way bad guys talked in 1940 movies. He says "jernt" and has a Rocky Graziano inflection. But there is an intensity to what he says that shines through the roughness. "You know, I know now that all my life this is what I was looking for, to relate to something outside myself. I work in Fortune's store in the Village now, and I come in two hours early and I close it an hour late. I need those customers. I talk to them and some of them come back and some even write me."

One night he was in the store when a college girl came in and started telling him that she was looking for a place to stay. She was leaving home because her father couldn't understand her. Chuck saw the possibilities. She was innocent and an easy score. "I could have taken advantage of her." But Chuck, too, is innocent. That's why they call him Billy Budd. So he sat there and talked to her about going back and confronting her father. "Did you ever tell him you loved him? Maybe he's as afraid to touch you as you are to touch him." And he told her about the greatest book he ever read, *The Diary of Anne Frank.* "There she is, going to the ovens, and she is still looking for the best in people." They talked for two hours, and then he put her on a bus back to Buffalo. A week later he got a letter from her boyfriend thanking him and expressing amazement that an ex-convict could have such compassion.

Chuck works in the store every day selling and arranging the display of prison-made artifacts, books, and posters. He is also going to school to qualify as a movie theater projectionist. He thinks it's funny that it takes six months of school to learn to be a projectionist and only two weeks of training to be a prison guard. Just about all his life is wrapped up in Fortune. David and Joe Calley, who works in the Fortune office, are the first real friends he has ever had. The store and the speaking engagements he goes on, he insists, make his world bigger than it's ever been before. It sounds believable. He knows that sooner or later he will have to squirm out a little from the comfortable protectiveness of Fortune. "I'm going to find out if I can do it on my own. Say, meet a girl someplace away from Fortune and deal with her on my own and not as a member of Fortune, but I have to keep confronting myself a little bit at a time."

That's the way Chuck talks now. Directly and abruptly. He can look at someone he has known only an hour and tell him, "God, you know, I am bursting with love. For years I was alone and kept everything locked up inside, but now I feel like I'm exploding with feeling." When he first started hanging around, it was different. He would stay back and while MacGregor and Mel Rivers joked and laughed, he'd do his typing. Gradually, when a convict would come in from upstate, Chuck would show him where the clothes were or help him make phone calls for job interviews or help get the guy a room. And then one day, a couple of weeks after he had started coming around, David asked him to go with a panel that was speaking at a Long Island high school. Chuck was in the audience as David and four of his ex-cons started talking about the system of prison brutality. They told how all their decision-making had been taken away from them, how the system dehumanized them and the guards too, so that men were no longer dealing with each other as human beings but as nameless, soulless bodies. They described prison as a society where the strong and the brutal rose to the top over a heap of weaker, subjugated men. When it was over, the audience sat quiet, impressed. There were a few timid questions about food and sex inside, and one probable Young American for Freedom asked what the panel thought should be done with killers, robbers, and others who were threats to society. Mel Rivers answered that such people should certainly be removed from society's midst, but that while they were away they should be helped to change. "All of those guys are going to come out someday, and the way they're coming out now is worse than the way they went in." A young girl, shaken by what she had heard, asked, "Is there anything that inmates can do to change things?" David answered saying that Chuck, sitting in the audience, might be able to talk about that. And then Chuck rose, surprised that he wasn't nervous, and with his thick, boxy fingers twined in a clasp before him, he started to talk.

"I had been at Comstock doing seven to twelve for armed robbery, and the prison was running smoothly, not well, but smoothly. But then the Republicans lost the governor's election and they brought in a new warden. They shipped out a lot of the older inmates and brought in a new staff, and they were going to run things tight. There was a new order. Small infractions were being punished harshly. They were picking out weak, small guys for no reason and sending them to the hole. They were using their sticks all the time. The food got worse. After a while, 162 of us out of maybe 1,200 decided to do something. We called a strike and said we weren't going to come in from the yard until they heard our grievances. We stayed out for sixteen hours, and after they threatened to beat us and starve us, and after they gave us some phony promises we wouldn't buy, they called in the state troopers. They came in with shotguns and started rounding us up. One guy fell against a trooper and his gun went off, hitting another trooper in the leg. That was all they needed. They cleared out a wing of the prison and put us in tiers. Then, one by one, they came for the guys. They were all stripped down naked, and you could hear them screaming as they were taken off. Since me and another guy were the spokesmen, they saved us for last. I kept wishing they would come and get it over with, but it lasted hours. Finally they came, and with me handcuffed they dragged me down to the center where most of the prison population could watch. They came at me with billies and sticks, about twenty of them. I don't know how long it was, maybe fifteen minutes. The deputy kept shouting not to hit in the head. Then they put us in strip cells. Nothing but a mattress. Nothing to read. One meal every two days. After a week you stink like an animal. Maybe twenty-five guys cracked up and were sent to hospitals. I survived only because I kept killing them in my head, over and over. Then they got us out and they used the same damn razor to shave all of us. I was not a revolutionary, my motives were simple. I wanted to get transferred and I was willing to take whatever they gave to get someplace else, but that's what happens when you try to change things. When my prayers were answered and they shifted the whole lot of us to Dannemora, they were polite. All they said was if there's any trouble here, we're going to kill you. And I believed them."

It was the best part of the discussion, and Chuck became a regular on the speaking engagements. Some of the others had been doing it so long that they were cued in to each other's responses. But Chuck was new and it was all coming out. He read in the mornings and then started working at the store, at first for nothing and then, when his compensation ran out, for $90 a week. David got him enrolled in a program to train him as a movie projectionist. After work he would go to David's house, and the stream that started at the high school kept on rolling. Direct, no self-pity, but the story had to come out.

A week after that first discussion, he spent hours telling David about his first sixteen years. David cried when he heard it, and that's when he started calling Chuck Billy Budd. They were drinking beer, and Chuck was bubbling about some people he had met in the store, a family from out of town, sightseeing in the Village. They were saying how frightened they had been coming to New York after reading about muggers and street crime, but everyone was so nice to them and here they were in a store run by ex-convicts. He told them he had been the world's worst stickup man, who took his first arrest on a two-cent burglary, and they had laughed and ended up buying some love beads for the people back home. They seemed, said Chuck, like a warm, fine family, and the woman, a little plump with crinkly eyes, was like the mother he had invented.

It was in 1940 that he first started thinking about that mother. He was eleven years old and had just been sent to the State Training School for Boys at Warwick. Four years before that, he had been taken away from the woman who had cared for him for the first seven years of his life. There was a house out in Queens with a car and a nice man and woman. The man got a swelling on his neck and died, and then another woman came and took him to an orphanage. Two years later he went to another orphanage. There were priests and nuns there, and he remembers trying to find out what he was being punished for and what had happened to his mother, the lady in Queens. One day he stole a cigarette lighter and, while he was playing with it, set a small fire he put out himself. The priests brought him to court and he was ruled an incorrigible and sent to Warwick, the youngest child there. Soon after he arrived, he was taken to a social worker. "When," he asked, "can I go home to my mother?" "You have no mother; the woman in Queens is not your mother," the social worker told him. "You were a foster child and the woman's husband died and you had to be taken away."

That's when he started inventing his mother. Sometimes he would tell the other kids about her. It was hard to pretend because the other kids would be allowed to go home on weekend passes every once in a while, but he had no place to go. After two years, they, the people at Warwick, took pity and started letting him come to the city. He would sleep at Youth House, the detention center here. The rest of the time he was free, alone, but free. Twice he went to see the woman in Queens, who cried and held him. The rest of the time he would go to movies. He liked gangster pictures because he was starting to think of himself as a gangster. "I knew Pretty Boy Floyd's record like other kids know batting averages." Before he would take the bus back to Warwick, he would go to a supermarket and steal cookies and food to share with his friends. "All of them would come back with shopping bags and I was ashamed. I'd tell them the stuff was from my mother."

When he was fifteen, Catholic Charities got him another mother, a woman in the Bronx who took kids in for the money. Again he was alone. The neighborhood kids were afraid of him. He didn't play ball well. The kids in Warwick had respected him because he would break the rules. The black kids had taught him to box, and he fought well. The kids in the Bronx, though, kept teasing him and weren't impressed by the knife he carried. One day he went up to his room and hung himself. He screamed loud enough for the woman to hear. "It was a false attempt, but they sent me to a state hospital for fifteen months. I had nothing to do up there. There were no interviews, no therapy. That's where I really started thinking about my mother. I would lie in bed and figure out all kinds of noble reasons why she gave me away. How she didn't want to do it, but she had to to save the country. She was beautiful and kind, and she was looking for me but didn't know where I was."

Then, in the stream of endless seamless days, another social worker told him his real mother was alive. That she had given birth to him when she was sixteen and that his father was someone named Parisi. She gave him his mother's address. "I wrote her forty letters before I sent one. She wrote back sending ten dollars, and she said how sorry she was. She wrote she was going to visit me." There were no tears in Chuck's eyes as he told the story, and no weakness in his voice. But in one or two places he stammered. "The day they called my name to say I had a visitor, I was jumping out of my skin. I walked down the long hall, and there were two women in the sitting room. I went to one of them, I guess the prettier one, and held out my arms and said, 'Mom,' and she stepped back. Of course it was the other one." She cried, and Chuck wanted her to hold him, but she wouldn't or couldn't. She kept crying. "You know what I told her? I was so stupid. I wanted her to feel better. I said, 'Don't cry, Mom, we all make mistakes. Once I knocked up a girl.' I made it up to make her feel better, but, God, how I must have hurt her."

A few months after the visit he was released. His mother said he could not come to live with her. She was married and had two children. He could visit. She would introduce him as her cousin. He was sixteen years old, and after two foster homes, two orphanages, one reformatory, one suicide attempt, and one mental hospital, he was free and on his own and lonely as he had ever been.

Up to that time he had never been inside a police station. This was to change quickly. Sometimes the men of Fortune describe their criminal pasts with a kind of bravado. MacGregor, for instance, talks about how sick he was. So sick that he used to enjoy stomping his mugging victims. He remembers one Chinese man he robbed, and he tells of his feeling of relief when he realized the man did not know judo. "I just jumped on him and jumped on him and it felt good." The point of all this, they say, is that neither the courts nor the prisons did anything for the sickness, and that for every one of the motivated people who walk into Fortune there are thousands who are on a treadmill in and out of jail. Chuck explained one night over beers that he didn't really become diseased until he got a gun. There was a man there from the Rand Corporation, and he was asking the stickup men how they operated. He wanted to know whether the presence of police in the area acted as a deterrent. He was working on a project to see what police procedures could be adopted to lessen crime. With his guttural precision, Chuck told him, "Look, I'm supposed to be an intelligent guy, and I mean I always considered myself intelligent, but when I think back, I was real stupid. I knew all the ways in which the great gangsters operated. They were my heroes, but whenever I went out to knock a place off, I never cased it, I never thought of how to get away, I didn't care who was in it. I'd just walk down a street looking and then I'd walk into the first bar or restaurant I found. I used to hate to admit it, but my first arrest was for a two-cent burglary."

He had come back from the mental hospital, and was working as a dishwasher in midtown for $22 a week. He lived in a rented room for which he paid $12 a week. He knew no one his age and had no friends. He kept thinking of the stories he had heard at Warwick, and he thought money was the answer. What he would do was go into bars very late and hide in the men's room after closing. Then he'd clean out the till. Meanwhile he was still washing dishes. One night he went up to the Bronx and broke into a bar. The place had been burgled so often that they kept only two cents in the register. He went after the jukebox, and as he was trying to take the cover off with his hands, a piece of glass broke and gashed his palm. He was frustrated and bleeding, and as he walked out on the street he saw a cab and flagged it down. But it wasn't a cab, it was a police car. He invented a story on the spot, how he had cut himself on a piece of metal sticking out of a car. They took him to the hospital where he was sewn up. But he had given the police his real name and address, and when the bar owners reported the burglary the next day, the police came to get him. He got two years, during which he got his high school equivalency certificate on a correspondence course. Now he came out to another rented room and a factory job in Queens. The work was mechanical and he felt boxed in, but he stayed with it. One day he answered an ad for a managerial trainee for a large supermarket chain. He faked his past, saying he was a Korean War veteran and had a year of college. The interviewer told him he seemed to be exactly what they were looking for. Chuck checked in with his parole officer to say he was switching jobs. The man asked him how he had gotten the job, and Chuck confessed to altering his background. The parole officer said he couldn't take the job.

Chuck felt himself going crazy. "What kind of bullshit is that? The P.O. wants to keep me in prison forever, only the prison is out on the street." He started stealing that night. He and an acquaintance he met would cruise dark suburban streets and break into parked cars. They were looking for salesmen's cases, and once they got 400 Piaget watches. Another time they spotted a car with a police jacket in the back. His partner wanted the badge. Chuck figured there had to be a gun somewhere, and he found it in the glove compartment. At that time he used to dress in slick black pants, a black shirt, a white tie, and a gray sport jacket. He wore a wide-brimmed hat over his eyes. Whatever he stole, he peddled to a fence who ran a barbershop around Madison Square Garden, getting about 10 percent of what it was worth. He had money now, but he was starting to gamble very heavily. "I thought that made me important. I was big when I was winning, and then I guess I had to lose it all. In a way I thought that made me big too, being able to blow my roll." To support his gambling he increased his haul. He would prowl around in the garment center in the late afternoon, picking up parcels left on the sidewalks by parcel post services or the mail. Sometimes it was a thousand ties, sometimes it might be a fur coat. His fence started calling him "the Producer" because he was always able to get something. Then, after eight months of freedom, he was arrested by postal inspectors and sent to the federal detention center to stand trial. He remembers he met Waxy Gordon there, and he felt awe at being near one of his heroes. After pleading guilty, he got a year at Chillicothe. He came there with a good reputation. The inmates made things easy for him and got him a good clerical job. He trained for a bout against the black middleweight champion. He lost the fight, but put up a good battle. The blacks liked him and so did the whites. He kept on listening to crime stories, and when he came out he felt he had graduated. He quickly got a gun.

"I was living on the East Side and hanging out on the West Side, and the first night I went out with the gun I was scared. I knew that the trick was in the delivery. You have to sound very brutal. Use a lot of obscenities. I walked into this place and when I got my gun out I calmed down.

I could see the bartender was deciding whether he should make a move. 'Don't do anything heroic,' I told him. And I took his money and made the three customers lie down and took their wallets. I don't know how to describe the feeling. It was like when I played football in the joint. Before the game you were all tight, but the first time you were hit, the feeling spread out from your gut and everything was all right. The bar I knocked off was two blocks from my house, and I just walked up there. Next day I couldn't wait to get the papers and there it was in the *Post*, a small article that I cut out."

He started going out two or three nights a week hitting places, always alone. At a bar he met a young divorcée, a schoolteacher, and for a few months he lived with her. "It wasn't love, we just both had large sexual appetites. But she was intelligent, and she started me reading. It was probably the least lonely period for me until I found Fortune." But that ended and he was gambling. At the bar he hung around in, he would tell some of the people what he had been doing. One of them was a stool pigeon who set him up. They picked him up as he was going to a card game. They found the gun he was carrying and they asked him where the other two were. Only the guy at the bar knew he had three guns. They brought in his victims to identify him. With his broken nose, gray eyes, and curly hair, Chuck is not nondescript. There was no point in denying anything. He waived a trial and pleaded guilty. That's when he went to Comstock, and then on to Dannemora.

Toward the end of his eight-year term, Chuck became withdrawn. He started hanging around less with the hardened cases and he didn't join in the stories. He would wonder sometimes what other life there was. He started reading a book a day and got subscriptions to *Life, Time,* and *Newsweek.* When he got out, he took a series of menial jobs. There was another rented room. And again the feelings of loneliness. He was, he says, starting to get afraid. It wasn't long before he got a gun. He would stay in his room holding it, and he remembers asking himself, "How crazy are you? You know you hate the walls, hate them worse than anything, but you really want to go back." "I was realizing that I was less lonely inside than out, and I was realizing how horrible that was."

Now, when he started pulling stickups, he had only one thing in mind. He didn't want to go back upstate. He didn't want to see the same faces and tell the same stories. He started taking the Hudson tubes, two, three nights a week, to Hoboken and Jersey City, and hitting the tough little neighborhood bars. He had been out about six months when the police spotted him leaving a place. He panicked, pointed his gun at a motorist, and forced the man to drive him away. En route he knew it was over and threw the gun out of the car. He doesn't think he could have shot the driver, but he thinks he could have shot bartenders. He was put in Essex County House of Detention. Kayo Koenigsberg was there at the time, but Chuck didn't even want to see him. He again pleaded guilty, but before sentence was passed the judge asked the defendant if he had anything to say. With pain and confusion on his open face, Chuck told the judge that he knew he was a menace and that he had to be put away. He said he did not know why, exactly, he did the things he did. All he was asking for was to be given some help this time. He wanted to see a psychiatrist. The judge, a man named Rosen, whom Chuck thinks of in the same way that he thinks of David, said he would take the matter under advisement. After studying Chuck's record, he passed sentence. Five to seven at Trenton, with the recommendation that the prisoner be given psychiatric help.

According to the Fortune Society, Trenton was probably the worst of the northern prisons. Drugs, homosexuality, and gambling were all carried out openly, with the support of the administration. These things existed in the other places too, but they were clandestine. Chuck quickly fell in with the operation. A year went by and he hadn't seen a psychiatrist. He opened up a bookmaking operation and was taking in two hundred packs of cigarettes a day. One day he went to sick call and asked to see a psychiatrist. The orderly told him there weren't any, and did he want to be sent to a state hospital. On his way back, he saw a deputy warden. "Dep, I've got problems. I've got to see someone, talk about it." The deputy laughed. "We've all got problems. Why don't you get yourself an old lady?"—meaning a homosexual partner.

Chuck invested his cigarette hoard in a letter. For five cartons he got a guard to kite a message to Judge Rosen, explaining that he was receiving no treatment. A month later he became one of sixteen men in the large prison to get psychiatric help. For six months he would go weekly to talk to a young doctor. "The guy would never say anything. I'd ask him questions, and he'd say nothing. But if he got sick a week, I'd be depressed. I built my time around those sessions. I could feel myself beginning to feel. It was the first time I talked to someone and it was like when I had the gun, the feeling swelling up inside me." He came up before the parole board after five, and they really worked him over. He knew that he was closer to being ready for the outside than he had ever been. He came back from the session convinced he hadn't made it. Then the word came. He was paroled. Not only that, but from a friend who worked in the office he learned that the board had ruled that his chances for readjustment were "excellent." Usually they write "undetermined." But there was another hurdle. New York wanted him for parole violation. He had hoped they would waive it in the light of his genuine reformation. They didn't. He got two more back at Dannemora. He stayed away from things. If he saw brutality, he didn't let it touch him, he sealed himself off from prison. And then, at the age of thirty-five, he got out, knowing, really knowing, that he never wanted to go back in. He got the job as a roofer and he had his room. He couldn't tell the people he worked for who he was or what he had been. The need to pretend was keeping him from friends. Then he saw MacGregor, and he came down to Fortune.

He can tell his story now, and he wants to tell it: not for sympathy or romance, but to tell himself who Chuck Bergansky is. When the letters come in, like the one from the kid at Rikers Island who burns himself with a cigarette and is pleased that he still can feel pain, Chuck can answer. When Chuck goes out to talk, he speaks of the need for prison reform, and he means what he says. But there is a greater meaning for him. There are faces looking at him and people wanting to be touched and people who will touch him. When he walked through the door at Fortune, he says, he was born.

The More Things Change . . .

The most important thing about the area that surrounds Forsyth Street on New York's Lower East Side is that for eighty years it has been part of somebody's slum or ghetto. The dumbbell tenements were built to be slums and, of course, they have deteriorated. When Harlem and Bedford-Stuyvesant and the other areas that are the clichés of urban blight and white guilt were suburban outcroppings, Forsyth and the streets around it were already festering in the muck of slum poverty. There were then as there are now rats, disease, overcrowding, and frustration. The Irish were there first, but they and their grandchildren have long since left for the two-story houses of Bailey Avenue in the Bronx and the self-respect of Bay Ridge. Then the Jews were its occupiers and captives, but except for a few old-timers and a few delicatessens still around, they too have gone, absorbing Forsyth Street into a mythology of hard work, cooperative effort, and dedication that brought about the exodus from poverty. Now the houses along the strip are filled with Puerto Ricans. Just north of Forsyth at the intersection of Allen and Houston is a square named for Isaac Loeb Peretz, the Yiddish playwright. The kids around the area call it Perez Square.

The stories of the older generations of Forsyth's inhabitants have been written many times over. Some have been burnished with a romantic nostalgia. Certainly not everything about the life there then was rats and filth, nor is it today. But despite the protestations of many who lived through Forsyth's middle slum period, there was crime, there was early death, and there was misery. That time has been recorded in books and even musical comedies. The stories of the *jíbaros* from Puerto Rico is being acted out in spontaneous dramas. Someday, perhaps, their grandchildren will think of it in terms of *West Side Story*.

Before the turn of the century, a well-to-do Jewish girl from Cincinnati named Lillian Wald established the Henry Street Settlement House, with a visiting nurse service. She kept careful notes of the calls she made on needy residents. These manuscripts are now in a special collection at the New York Public Library. This is her account of one such visit on July 2, 1895: "Climbing the stairs in search of Mrs. Schwartz (the mother of a child with ophthalmia), found terrible filth everywhere. Stair filled with slops, floor reeking. I went into every room in the front and rear tenement and set the dwellers to sweeping, cleaning and burning refuse. In some rooms swill thrown on floor, vessels standing in rooms unemptied from the night's use." Much of the area covered by Mrs. Wald on her rounds has been torn down and replaced by public housing with its own special, newer miseries. But along Allen, Rivington, and Stanton streets the houses are the

Michael T. Kaufman

same as the ones she saw. They have been revised, refurbished, and rehabilitated. Indoor plumbing has been added, but they still reek.

Mrs. Eleutheria Valdez lives in a four-room apartment at 170 Forsyth Street for which she pays $92.50 a month. The floors and the stairs pitch like the hatchways of a freighter in trouble. The pipes leak and contaminated water drips, filling the house with the smell of piss. In her apartment, laundry is strung out on lines that crisscross the living room. There is a refrigerator, but it doesn't work, and the bath has been stopped up for months. A chicken kept as a pet by Mrs. Valdez's son struts nonchalantly on the furniture and leaves its droppings on layers of linoleum that signify generations of dwellers like the stratifications of sedimentary rock. The chicken represents something new. The residents are *jíbaros*—a term akin to *hillbilly* that once meant "bumpkin" but now is used with pride. They are hill people, from remote villages where agriculture and chickens made sense. In a very short span they have been thrown into the vortex of the world's most complicated and commercial city. Many of the Jews, too, came from villages, and some were farmers; but they had, for centuries, understood commerce. There is another difference in Mrs. Valdez's apartment—the big television set that dominates the room. The shriveled, fifty-year-old woman has been here three years and she speaks English poorly, but she can recognize five different kinds of deodorants, and she can tell a Ford from a Chevrolet, and she knows she has a friend at Chase Manhattan, but she doesn't know where that is. Her children have learned that most Americans live in houses with picket fences and have fathers who work. The Jews really didn't know who lived on Thirty-fourth Street, and they didn't much care. It was enough to know that Romanian Jews were on Allen, and

152

Russian Jews were south of Delancey, and the Irish were west of the Bowery. It was slightly more possible then not to know you were poor.

Mrs. Rosalia Gomez lives just below Mrs. Valdez, and she pays $106.33 for her apartment. The interior walls have been torn down so that only three counter-high barriers separate its four rooms. In a way that's good, because the five children can stay in bed and watch TV in the main room. They are sick a lot and miss school often, so that the arrangement is beneficial. Except for the beds and the set, there is no furniture. The refrigerator does not work, and Mrs. Gomez sends one of the kids down to buy a quart of milk every morning for breakfast. She used to work in the garment center, operating a sewing machine, but the aunt who watched the children went back to Puerto Rico, so now she has to stay home and is on welfare.

Sir Jacob Epstein, the sculptor, grew up a few blocks from the Gomezes' house. In his autobiography, *Let There Be Sculpture*, he describes the life there in the 1880s:

> This Hester Street and its surrounding streets were the most densely populated of any city on earth, and looking back on it I realize what I owe to its crowded humanity. Its swarms of Russians, Poles, Italians, Greeks and Chinese lived as much in the streets as in crowded tenements; and the sights, sounds and smells had the vividness and sharp impact of an oriental city.

There is still a lot of action in the streets, partly because the streets, dirty as they are, are more comfortable than the houses. There are no roaches on the street, and in the summer the heat is a bit more bearable. Felix Merced is a large-boned twenty-six-year-old merchant seaman who knows all of the streets and most of the people on them. Felix has lived in the area all of his life. Since he's been at sea, he has circled the globe and stayed in many fine places. He has flirted on the Riviera and got drunk on the Ginza, but this slum is home and always will be. It is where he wants to live. "There are rats here and garbage all over the street and junkies crawling in and out of buildings. But it's not bad. Like, man, everybody knows everybody, and if you need help, you don't have to ask. The guys I grew up with, we're as tight as brothers. Hell, we are brothers. Henry Ramos, he'll get me a job, or I'll get him one. His kids are like my own nephews and nieces." Felix paused in his bouncy stroll down Stanton Street to flirt with a pretty girl of about thirteen. "How did you ever get to be so beautiful?" he asked her. She blushed and told him to go back to sea. From the fourth-story window a heavy woman shouted down to him in Spanish, her face breaking into a grin. He shouted back. "Remember when we had that big freeze back in January? Well, the wind was blowing wicked and I turned the corner of Eldridge when I saw that big mama fall on the ice. Her packages went shooting up and she's trying to get to her feet. I come up and told her, 'What are you praying for, get off your knees, this ain't no church,' and I picked her up. Well, she just shouted down to tell me she isn't praying."

Felix is pretty happy with his life now. "I'm free. I can always get a job and I like to move around. For a while I worked developing film at a place where Henry got me a job. Then I got my seaman's papers and I shipped out. One time I hitchhiked to California to see what was out there. When I ran out of money, I shipped out there." He knows, though, that things could have turned out differently. "I was pretty wild, and some of the guys I ran with have wound up in jail or are stone junkies. I was doing some stealing—like we'd go into Yonah Shimmel's and grab a tray of knishes—and I was playing hooky. When I was ten, they put me into a 600 school, but that wasn't a school at all. You had to fight all the time. The bigger kids held up the little ones. I started staying away from there, too, which looked bad on my record. Well, I started coming around this church community center to play pool and that's where Father Janner got ahold of me." The priest is no longer in the area, having been reassigned to Louisiana, but according to Felix and his friend Henry he was the greatest man they had ever met. Said Felix, "He was tough but he was fair, and when I got caught breaking and entering when I was fourteen, he had me sent to a home run by the priests. They were tough, too, but goddamn it, that's what I needed. I started reading up there and I suddenly realized how scared I had been all my life, scared of trying, scared of failing. The more I read, the less scared I became."

As he continued the walk, Felix pointed to some bright murals of Aztec kings, palm trees, and beaches. Others, done in the same bold style, were abstracts. They covered the first stories of several buildings. "The guy that did those is called the Nomad. He's a junkie. You can catch him every afternoon on the corner waiting for his man to come around with the rest of them. He does these paintings to feed his habit. Like, he'll come in and ask a storekeeper if he wants to make his place look sharp and then, for like $10 and the paint, he'll do one of these." One of these paintings, next to a bodega, is just around the corner from the house where Jacob Epstein had his first studio.

Hutchins Hapgood was one of the first outsiders to be captivated by the life of the Jewish ghetto. In his book *The Spirit of the Ghetto*, written in 1902, he described the attempts at acclimatization of the newly arrived immigrant, confronted by a strange land and an alien language:

His deeply rooted habits and the "worry of his daily bread" make him but little sensitive to the conditions of his new home. His imagination lives in the old country and he gets consolation in the old religion. He picks up only about a hundred phrases, which he pronounces in his own way. Some of his most important acquisitions are vinda (window), zieling (ceiling), never mind, all right, that'll do, politzman, and ein shon kind, ein reglar pitze (a pretty child, a regular picture).

At 207 Eldridge Street there is a storefront that has been converted to a nursery and day care center. It also doubles as a place for practice in English. It is run by the Mothers Club, fifteen women recently arrived from Puerto Rico. Mrs. Doris Cosme, the organizer of the project, explained the way the club works. The women each get $22.50 a month to pay for child care while they take special English classes in the morning, but they had trouble finding babysitters. So they formed the club and pay in their money, which is used for rent and to hire a regular teacher. Some of the mothers have finished the English course and now work, paying a part of their salary to the cooperative day care center. There is a kitchen in the place to provide hot meals for the children. And there are cots so the youngsters can nap. When the mothers join they must abide by the single rule: no Spanish. All conversation must be in English. The words they learned first were "apartment," "super," "sewing machine," and "job."

Lincoln Steffens was another journalist fascinated by the life of the old ghetto. In his autobiography he described how one day, while he was a young police reporter in the 1890s, a mother blocked his path and began complaining bitterly about her children's behavior.

> She seized and pulled me up the stairs, weeping, into her clean, dark room, one room, where her three little girls were huddled at one rear window, from which they—and we—could see a prostitute serving a customer. "Da, se'n Sie, they are watching, always they watch. . . . My oldest girl says she will go into that business, when she grows up; she says it's a good business, easy and you dress and eat and live."

"The trouble with the kids now is that they are exposed to adulthood too early," says Henry Ramos, Felix Merced's buddy. He is twenty-seven years old and works as a community organizer for the local antipoverty program. "I was wild, I've been to reform school, but the first time I tasted whiskey I was eighteen. Today you see thirteen-year-old kids drunk on the street. The tiny ones start sniffing glue, and then they start on pot and after that cocaine and heroin. They see the junkies everywhere. The kids go to these dances and stay out late. Lots of times by the time a girl is sixteen, she's already got a belly."

If squalor has its own patterns, so too does prejudice. The rhetoric of bigotry has a familiar ring. On July 30, 1895, *The New York Times* ran this story about the Jews of the Lower East Side:

> A writer might go on for a week reciting the abominations of these people and still have much to tell. One of their greatest faults is that they have an utter disregard for law. There is a certain hour that they are required to set out their garbage and ash cans, but

they pay no attention to that. Filthy persons and clothing reeking with vermin are seen on every side. Many of these people are afflicted with sores and hundreds of them are nearly blind with sore eyes. Cleanliness is an unknown quantity to these people. They cannot be lifted to a higher plane because they do not want to be.

"Sometimes people call us names," said Mr. Ramos. "They say we are dirty and that all we came here for was to get welfare. What we really want is to work and get a better break for our kids."

None of this is meant to imply that Jewish and Puerto Rican cultures are synonymous. What I think I have seen in my rambles in the area is that there is a culture of need, and an alienation that sometimes supersedes national character, and that this culture has held Forsyth Street in its grip for nearly a century. I did not know the Jewish ghetto when it was roiling with humanity and frustration, so it is hard for me to say which group had it worse. Certainly indoor plumbing is an improvement. But in that earlier time there was a greater possibility for upward mobility. When there were no unions, you could start unions. A bright young punk could work his way up in crime; today that too is a closed corporation, and the best a hoodlum can hope for is to run numbers or peddle dope. The Jews had their religion, which was theirs. The Puerto Ricans come to an Irish-dominated Catholic Church in which they feel uncomfortable. Many leave it for Pentecostal congregations. Time has shaped the memories of what Hapgood and Steffens reported. The grandchildren of those who passed through the old ghetto often think of that time in terms of mother love and the desires of a people to improve their conditions. And so, in part, it must have been. And so, in part, it is today for the Puerto Ricans.

I would like to end this chapter with a letter I received after a shorter version of this chapter appeared in the *Times*. My correspondent was a woman from Brooklyn. "My dear young man," she began with a perception that is worthy of note since she not only guessed I am young, but also, as the letter will show, that I am Jewish. This despite the fact that 0.05 percent of all one-*f* and one-*n* Kaufmans are actually Parsees.

This is the typical, incredible, deprecatory Jewish "intellectual," insensitive, masochistic aberration. Such jewels of comparative relevant anals of prejudice! "they [Jews] throw garbage in the cans . . ." With your typewriter you wipe out the specific prejudice and causes historically reserved for Jews! You people won't even give us the benefit of our history. But you intellectual types *do* love such terms as prejudice, discrimination, minority, etc. With these semantics you are therefore able to compare the similarity and justification of past prejudice against Jews and the present general revulsion against Puerto Ricans. The comparison is as valid as may be the comparison between an elephant's front and its rear. It is neither true for aesthetic appearances, culture, way of life and moral behavior. The only stable thing that one can extract from your article is the observation of the compulsive Jewish intellectual neurosis, that looks at itself as a negative run-of-the-mill factor, only achieving positivity by comparing itself unfavorably with other peoples! This is the questionable image that you intellectuals want to portray of the Jewish masses to the Jewish people (and others). Jewish history gives very poor proof that such behavior on the part of our intellectuals has resulted in the aggrandizement of its history or of itself. Contrarily, assertive selfless Jewish intellectualism is the basic, root cause of its catastrophes, and its irretrievable historical position! This instigating neurosis is the Jewish curse, and nothing else. Where did you find, even in your myopic view, that Jews mugged, knifed and shot, took dope, terrorized storekeepers and vandalized everywhere. New Terminology ought to be invented for such Jews as yourself, such as would hold to derision the term intellectual.

I really like the woman's style, and it is always fun to hear from one's readers. As for an answer, maybe she can find it in the next chapter. It won't tell her anything about Jews, but she may learn something about Puerto Ricans.

Basta Ya!

The sun cut through an October haze, warming the bus-loads of activists who had descended upon the main street of Wrightstown, New Jersey. They had come, some five thousand of them, to rage against the military for its incarceration of some young soldiers in the stockade at Fort Dix, less than a mile away. In the milling crowd, slopped over from the street to supermarket parking lots, there were blue-haired Quaker ladies and middle-aged veterans of World War II, angry at the war in Vietnam. They were outnumbered by the young. Serious young men from the Catholic Peace Fellowship, sullen, noncommunicative Panthers, and helmeted Krazies holding high the black standard of anarchy. Off at one corner of one parking lot, a fiery redhead was instructing a woman's battalion in the use of six-foot-long cardboard poles. "We're not ready to use them as offensive weapons, swinging them from side to side like the Zenka Kuren. We're not that disciplined," she explained, referring to the Japanese militant organization, and then went on to say that each rank of four women should keep together by holding onto a single pole held before them. As she talked, girls walked through the crowd distributing plastic shower caps to be used as improvised gas masks, and they smeared Vaseline on each other's faces to protect from gas burns.

The plan was to walk down a public highway to the military reservation and then, somehow, to get onto the base itself. The leaders wanted to walk right up to the stockade, past the sign that said, "Fort Dix, the Home of the Ultimate Weapon," and past the other sign that said, "Ft. Dix, an Equal Opportunity Employer." "Equal Opportunity," said one black youth, "shit, it's more than equal, baby." The crowd was restless and wanted to start moving, but there had to be speeches first. The Panthers wanted money for a bail fund, and some GIs on leave talked of incipient rebellion on the bases around the country and in Vietnam. The crowd didn't really want to listen. They knew all that. They were starting to drift off toward the base when a heavyset kid in a huge afro that almost obscured the lurid purple beret he wore started shouting into the microphone. His name was Sabu and he was from something called the Young Lords Organization. "Dig it," he yelled. "What we've got to get down straight is that the motherfuckers who keep our motherfuckers in the motherfucking stockades are the same motherfuckers that kick our motherfuckers off the stoops in East Harlem." The succinct synthesis of oppression in our time drew laughter and cheers of "Right On!" from the crowd, which stopped moving. "And dig it," Sabu continued, "we, the Young Lords Organization, are saying we ain't going to take that shit anymore. The Man would put it down that spics are easygoing cats who will back down when the jive gets heavy. But that's a whole lot of shit. The Puerto Ricans have been revolutionaries all their lives." Sabu got a big hand and the crowd went off, shouting, "Free the Fort Dix 38" and "Ho, Ho, Ho Chi Minh, N.L.F. is gonna win." It was somewhat less patriotic, maybe, than "Soldier, soldier, where you been? Down in Wrightstown drinking gin," but there was, on the whole, a lot more feeling. The cordon of chanters got a few hundred yards onto the military reservation before it was sent scattering into retreat by tear gas. Everybody thought it was a success.

For the Young Lords of New York's barrio, it was a particularly important day. A few months earlier they had made their presence known to the Hispanic residents around 116th Street and Madison Avenue. On that day in New Jersey they had announced their arrival to the loose confederation of liberals, radicals, revolutionaries, and government agents generally referred to as "the movement." Within two months they would address themselves to a broader public. At the Fort Dix demonstration it was announced that the Lords had joined in the "Rainbow Coalition" with the Black Panthers and a Chicago-spawned group of émigré peckerwoods from Appalachia called the Young Patriots. Each of these units, linked by a Marxist-Leninist orientation, would work, it was said, among its own constituents to bring Power to the People—Black Power to the Black People, Puerto Rican Power to the Puerto Rican People, and White Power to the White People.

As far as New York was concerned, the Panthers were struggling. Their leadership was by and large in jail or in exile, and their ranks had been thinned by a recent purge. The Patriots opened up an office in Yorkville, hoping to organize working-class and poor whites. They succeeded in mustering some pretty girl college students, but they found their potential rank and file to be elusive. The

Lords, however, really got down to business. With flair and dedication they stormed into the largely apathetic, apolitical, disorganized, and disoriented life of the barrio. Like the Patriots, they had been conceived in Chicago. First they were a fighting gang, protecting its turf and its members from molestation by other street gangs. But then, several years ago, their leader, Cha Cha Jimenez, went to jail, and there he came in contact with Panthers and with the writings of Eldridge Cleaver. He came out and turned the Lords into a political organization, a force seeking control over community institutions. Word carried east, and in the spring of 1969 a small chapter was opened in New York. At first there was little more than the purple berets and a swarm of ideas: Puerto Rican nationalism, socialism, and cultural pride. Buttons were sold saying, "Yo tengo Puerto Rico en mi corazón" ("I have Puerto Rico in my heart"). The signature of the Young Lords began to appear spray-canned on the sides of tenements all over East Harlem. A storefront was rented on Madison Avenue near 110th Street, across the street from the Republican Club. It was kept open around the clock. Radical newspapers and the works of Che Guevara, Mao Tse-tung, Lenin, and Marx were on hand. Rap sessions and political discussions were held several times a week. New members were recruited. A leadership emerged and neighborhood people were encouraged to bring their problems with landlords and city agencies to the office. An ideology, studded with key phrases from Chairman Mao and Pedro Albizu-Campos, the Puerto Rican leftist *independista*, was developed.

Pablo Guzman was then a nineteen-year-old college student, thinking of becoming a lawyer some day. A product of the barrio, he had maintained his motivation through a series of strange schools. He spoke Spanish, but badly. He had not really thought too much about what it meant to be a Puerto Rican. That changed when he became a Lord. For one thing, the tall, bespectacled, and serious youth changed his name to Yoruba, in honor of his African heritage. Through studying with the others, he began to view the barrio as a captive nation, subjugated economically and culturally by the mother country. In time the Lords became his life and he was chosen as their minister of information. He quit school and gave himself to the struggle. A short time after the Fort Dix protest, he sat in the back room of the office and explained the context in which he saw oppression. The Puerto Ricans and the poor, in general, were being kept enslaved by the American myth. As long as the system could keep alive the belief in upward mobility, it would have a steady supply of low-paid, lethargic lackeys to feed its factories and build the profits of the establishment. It was, therefore, in the interests of the establishment to deny any expression of Latin culture. Racism was nothing else but a tool of the establishment to divide and conquer captive peoples; to set Puerto Rican against Negro, and poor white against both, keeping true and identical class aspirations from forming. Even something as destructive as the annihilation of the ghetto young through drugs was in effect condoned by the establishment, since it sapped and stupefied a potentially rebellious people. This was the reality that Yoruba together with the other Lords saw.

The first lesson of Marxism-Leninism, though, was to turn theory into practice. The theory was simple: a revolution led by the most oppressed elements in American society, blacks, Puerto Ricans, and poor whites. The task before them was to raise revolutionary consciousness, to destroy the American dream that kept them shackled to poverty. "To do that," the youthful minister explained, "we will use reformist tactics; but we will always set the revolutionary aim before the people. On reformist tactics alone, the Man can always co-opt you. He will give in here to protect there, but we just have to keep up the pressure." He pointed down the street to the chain of storefronts set up by the state and city agencies and eleemosynary institutions. "They're all poverty pimps, they think you can change the symptoms without changing the cause."

But wasn't revolution doomed if it came to struggle? Weren't there more oppressors than oppressed? he was asked. He smiled and answered, "How do I know that? Like Mao says, 'Everything my enemy affirms, I deny, and everything he denies, I affirm.' The Man says that only one out of every ten people is black, but how do I know that? Have I ever seen a census taker? Not only that, but in addition to the poor there are the culturally oppressed, the young, the students, the middle-class, who are becoming increasingly alienated." And then, after that somewhat quixotic appraisal (one that I thought he knew was quixotic), he said the thing that, to me, defined the Lords. "Like Che Guevara said, the basis of revolution is love, not a cold churchlike love, but a hot, fiery passionate love of your people."

By August the group had organized a cadre of several dozen. In addition to Yoruba, the leadership included Juan Gonzalez, who had been one of the leaders of the Columbia University uprising of 1968 and was now minister of education, and Felipe Luciano, a twenty-two-year-old poet and the president of the Lords. Decisions were made by a Central Committee that included these and a few others. Late in the month the group planned and executed its first major transference of theory into practice. Early one morning, before dawn broke, bands of Lords working in twos and threes moved stealthily down the streets of East Harlem, taking the garbage that had accumulated in front of the houses and piling it on the thoroughfares. The heaps of putrefying trash and papers blocked traffic on Madison and Fifth avenues. Circulars in Spanish and English were distributed to explain the action. As the residents know, the leaflets said, the pickup of refuse in East Harlem is abysmal. Sometimes days go by without sanitation trucks making their rounds. Bags of garbage age in front of the houses, and at night rats scavenge with impunity. The Young Lords served notice that, unless steps were taken to bring about regular garbage removal, the refuse would be periodically scattered on the streets, blocking traffic on the streets used by the Man's cars and trucks. It was also pointed out, as part of raising the revolutionary consciousness, that there was no problem in collecting garbage south of Ninety-sixth Street, where the rich people lived. The campaign brought the Lords some recruits, some enemies, and some friends. There was, however, an immediate improvement in garbage pickups.

As the summer ended, the Lords established a small breakfast and lunch program, providing warm meals to some twenty youngsters at Emmaus House, a Christian commune and house of hospitality on East 116th Street, but they were looking for some issues that would put them in direct contact with a large part of the community. They found it in pica. This is a condition that abounds in regions where there is hunger. Small children who do not get enough to eat put all sorts of things in their mouths. In some cases they eat peeling paint from their apartments and hallways. Sometimes this paint contains lead, and if it does, the child is in great danger. Lead poisoning can in some cases be fatal; more often it results in severe brain damage. If the condition is not caught by the time the child is seven, he may well be doomed to progressive retardation. The city council had taken steps to combat this, passing a law forbidding the use of lead paints. But underneath the newer coats that covered the houses of the barrio, the lethal layers remained. The city had also obtained as a gift from a pharmaceutical laboratory more than 10,000 kits to be used in testing for lead poisoning, but there was no money allocated for the testing. The Lords contacted some ideologically leftist medical students and obtained the kits from the city. Then, for months, they set out in teams of three, going from door to door, administering the tests. They were polite and solicitous. They walked into the overflowing warrens, ran their tests, and found about twelve children with signs of lead poisoning. These children were treated and saved. Along the way they also established themselves as friends of the community. They informed the residents about their health program, how they wanted Metropolitan Hospital to respond to the needs of neighborhood people, why medical care should be the right of every person. They said they wanted community control of the hospital, and they began organizing young doctors and unskilled hospital workers.

So far they had moved cautiously. The garbage campaign was short and relatively successful. The lead poisoning tests had extended their credentials. Now the stage was set for a new and more serious confrontation. On the corner of 111th Street and Lexington Avenue is a red brick building with a steeply pitched roof. This is the First Spanish Methodist Church, with a congregation of about 180. The parishioners are, by and large, old or middle-aged. They are neat and thrifty and generally pietistic. When the old church burned down five years ago, they volunteered their time and their money to build the new one. The building that rose was a monument to their devotion, and they regard it with pride. In addition to the chapel, which looks like the hold of an ark, there are several offices, six or seven classrooms, and two large meeting halls. On Sundays the church was alive with song and prayer, but the rest of the week it remained locked and unused. Since it occupied a plot of land in the very center of Spanish Harlem, and since it had a good deal of unused space, the Lords thought it would be an ideal place for a number of their proposed community programs.

That, at least, was their story. There are some members of the congregation and some community people who think the Lords' motives were less pragmatic and much more Byzantine. They argue that the whole campaign was intended to polarize the community, mobilizing support by attacking a very weak and unresponsive institution, and that the Lords never really cared whether or not they would be permitted to use the facilities. In a sense, some of the Lords would agree with this estimate, saying that the struggle against the church did raise revolutionary consciousness and that the reformist issue of free hot breakfasts, as laudatory as it was, simply raised the questions of what was a church, who owned it, and whom should it serve.

They began by writing a letter to the minister and the board of directors, asking for a meeting to discuss certain demands, which included permission to use the meeting halls for free breakfasts, a day care center, and a "liberation school." The Lords say they never received a response. They also say that when they attempted to go to the church to meet with the board they were turned back by policemen posted at the door. Yet even before the conflict hardened, both sides viewed each other with less than good faith. To the Lords, the minister of the church, Dr. Humberto Carranzana, was a *gusano*, a worm. He was a

Cuban, who had fled the Castro regime. "When we say *gusano*, it means the lowest form of Latin you can think of." The young activists saw the congregants as hardworking, sober people, many of whom had already left the barrio to live elsewhere. For Dr. Carranzana, the cadre of long-haired youth in the military dress and berets, with their lapel pins of the silhouetted profile of Mao Tse-tung, represented a fearful horror. In the pietistic tradition of Latin protestantism, he saw his mission as spiritual adviser to the faithful. He preached and he counseled, and this godless rabble had no place in his church.

Having failed in their approach to him and the board of directors, the Lords struck out on another tack. Early in October they began appearing at the Sunday services. About forty of them would enter and take seats in adjoining pews. During the services they would sit quite still and well-behaved. When the regular congregants sang hymns, they would sit mute. After services they tried to persuade the congregation to support them. At the end of one of these services, one who speaks Spanish better than most of the others, David Perez, rose and told the parishioners that the Lords felt it was criminal that they had this building and the space and that it was not being used to feed the hungry and clothe the poor. He said the group was not asking for any money, simply for the space to run its programs. He implored them to bring pressure on the pastor to respond to their demands. As he spoke, there were cries of "*Satanás!* [devil]" from the pews, and one large woman sank to her knees praying and crying. The pastor and most of the congregation filed out as Perez talked. The Lords promised to return and to keep returning until the church leaders would meet with them.

Meanwhile, they were coordinating their campaign. The word went out to the movement; financial support was being raised. A group of lawyers, young and committed to social change, was empaneled. Discussions were attempted with the Methodist Bishop Lloyd C. Wicke. At first these discussions seemed promising. The bishop, through his aides, acknowledged that the Spanish church had remained all too aloof from the community around it, and that social programs were needed. But still Dr. Carranzana refused to meet with what he felt to be Communist invaders of his church. They kept coming back each Sunday.

Then on a December Sunday the conflict was escalated. It is very hard to say by whom. The Lords arrived that morning as usual, only now their numbers were swelled with supporters from both within and outside of the barrio. Some Panthers and some members of the Patriots were present. There were several policemen outside, and in the congregation, dressed in civilian clothes, was Arthur Baller, the captain of the local precinct, who had been invited to attend by the minister. Toward the end of the service, one of the Lords rose to try again to convince the congregation. As he started to speak, the organist began playing and the congregation rose and sought to drown out the speaker with its song. That much everybody agrees on. At that point, says Dr. Carranzana, the Lords surged and knocked over a guard rail. The police who were outside were called. Dr. Carranzana said an officer ordered the Lords out and that they began fighting with the police. Captain Baller said that one youth swung a pipe at him but missed. The Lords' story differs. They admit they fought the police, but only to protect themselves and their women. They contend that the police burst in and immediately began swinging sticks, knocking their people on the head. This version was supported by a young Catholic priest from Emmaus House who, admittedly, was sympa-

171

thetic to the Lords. "They just came in and started club-
bing everyone in sight. Blood was spilled and there were
screams all over." By the time the church was cleared, thirteen Lords had been arrested on charges ranging from
criminal trespass to assault on an officer. Felipe Luciano
was among those seized. In the fray he had his arm broken
and his head split. The cast he wore through the rest of the
confrontation served as a banner for the struggle. At the
police station that day, Dr. Carranzana made the only
public comment he was to give during the month that his
church was to be in turmoil. "This community knows us.
Our church has been on this corner for fifty years. We re-
built the church. We paid the bills. This is our church. No
one has the right to deprive people of their place to worship. All the newspapers ever talk about is the breakfast
program, the breakfast program. Not every church can
have programs, and we can't have dealings with Commu-
nists."

For the Lords' part, Yoruba announced that the blood
that was spilled in the church would only intensify commitment and that the Lords would return, Sunday after
Sunday, until the church acceded to their demands. Meanwhile, Yoruba turned into a public relations wizard. He
got the names of television and newspaper reporters. His
dealings with the press were efficient and proper. Unlike
some leftist groups that publicly disparage the "bourgeois
press," the Lords were constantly available to reporters.
Despite an earlier proclaimed fear of "liberals," who, they
said, "want to play us off as the good guys and make the
Panthers the bad guys," they garnered support from what
they might have regarded as "poverty pimp" circles a few
weeks earlier.

On the Sunday after the arrests, the little church was
filled beyond capacity. There were perhaps eighty congre-

gants, engulfed by some two hundred supporters of the Lords, among whom were bearded whites and young women with peace buttons. Also present and sympathetic were Elinor Guggenheimer, a former member of the planning commission who had had a long interest in day care centers; Carter Burden, the rich, polished, and Waspy councilman, who brought along his wife, Amanda, hardly La Pasionaria. There was also Arnaldo Segarra, the mayor's personal envoy to the Puerto Ricans. Police cars and several patrolmen were stationed outside. But strangely there was little tension. Several Lords posted themselves around the large decorated Christmas tree in the rear of the chapel, making sure that no one brushed into it in the crush. When the congregation rose to sing, it was joined by many of the visitors. At the door a woman member of the choir approached one of the Lords, saying, "I want to apologize. I don't know if you remember, but I really pushed you last week. I was so mad. But all week long my sister has been talking to me, and I know you people are really interested and your programs are necessary. I'm sorry," and she offered her hand. The Lord, an earringed youth named Henry, answered, "That's all right, sister. That's why we keep coming back." The choir singer was one of a group of young people who, in the last week since the fighting, had sought to take a middle position and moderate the dispute. "Our position is that the breakfast program is good and that the Lords are in a position to carry it out, but what we don't want is for them preaching their views here. We won't preach Christ to them, but they shouldn't preach socialism to us," said Maria Valdes.

Meanwhile, negotiations with the Methodist Church had broken down completely. The church's superintendent, Dr. Wesley G. Osborne, was present at the church that Sunday; but when Daniel Myers, a volunteer lawyer, tried to talk about renewing discussions, he turned away. "When we thought that you were actually interested in some kind of community action programs, there was some purpose to discussions, but now all you seem to be interested in is getting publicity for yourselves." Later he explained that the church was willing to launch its own programs, but that these things took money. New bathrooms would have to be built if a day care center was to be provided because of city building regulation codes. "We are going to do it ourselves. To let any group dictate like this could encourage other efforts by fringe groups, for instance, efforts by those who want to put in segregated schools—for the community good. There are plenty of Hell's Angels and fascist groups who would be delighted to take the churches over." The Lords countered these arguments simply by saying that the churches are not now responding to real needs, and that they were prepared to feed the hungry. The tactic was effective.

Yoruba did his work well in scores of television interviews. To questions of whether the Lords were Maoist he replied with assurance, no, they were not, they were eclectic. Yes, they read Mao, but they also read Thomas Jefferson and the Federalists and they took what applied from many sources. The point, he kept stressing, was that the people of the slums had been socialists for generations. They knew all about sharing and giving to each other, and all they were seeking to do was to feed the hungry children. Who could be opposed to that? But the broader issue was outlined by Geraldo Rivera, one of the battery of volunteer lawyers. "This is the first battle in the war to make organized religion more relevant to the needs of poor people. When a church puts itself up as a House of God, it must follow its traditional role of helping the poor." As for the claim that it will undertake its own programs: "That's a put-up job. I won't believe the church until I see movement, and I doubt we will ever see movement."

Meanwhile, inside the church on that snowy December Sunday, the Lords again tried to reach the parishioners after the sermon was delivered. Juan Gonzalez said the young people in the congregation had expressed a desire for compromise, and that they had arranged a meeting between the Lords and the church elders to take place immediately after the service. He asked the supporters to stay in the chapel until the meeting was over. Two hours later he emerged to say that nothing had been achieved, and that the elders were still referring to the Lords as *Satanás*. He asked that the backers return in force on the next Sunday and the Sunday after that, "for as long as it takes."

By now the story had spread far beyond the confines of the barrio. Yoruba was appearing almost nightly on various news shows, articulately stressing the point that the Lords were interested in serving the people, and cleverly parrying questions about their supposed Maoist organization. On several programs he was also asked whether his group concurred with the Panthers' view that the citizenry should be armed. Here, too, his answer was clever. He pointed out that the Lords were alert to the menace of adventurism. They considered the Weathermen, for example, as "Custeristic fools." He said he thought that the actions of the SDS faction, who believed in open warfare on police, were suicidal and doomed because, unlike the Lords and the Panthers, they were not rooted in any oppressed class. "We have not battled with the police unless we're attacked first. We realize that the police are being used." Privately, he and the other Lords said they had not yet found it necessary to arm themselves, although they were keeping their options open.

What the Lords succeeded in doing was mounting a superb public relations job. They were young and vital and they projected that image. In all their appearances, they kept using the words *humanity* and *humanism*. They kept talking about coming together, learning of their common culture, and affirming a common humanity. As they walked down the street together, or ate in the steamy little restaurants of East Harlem, they gave evidence to their spirit. They were musketeers battling the forces of oppression, with arms locked around each other. They were Che and Fidel up in the hills, and Mao on the Long March. Revolution was exhilarating, and brotherhood was manifest. The meetings cropped up almost spontaneously and they held their conferences on street corners. Most of the group seemed to be engaged existentially. Some, like Juan Gonzalez, may have been more cunning and farseeing. Once a white moderate came up to Juan in the church and said he had been captivated by their handling of the situation, particularly because, of all the movement groups, they alone had shown "a humanism that transcended their dogma." Juan smiled and answered, "Yes, for the time being."

At services on December 21, the small church was again mobbed. In addition to the cadre of forty Lords and several hundred supporters, there were also dozens of newsmen, including a television crew from Sweden. On cue, as the service drew toward an end and the last notes of the last hymn died away, the Lords attempted to engage the minister in dialogue. He attempted to shut them off, but the audience, largely stacked against him, booed, and the Lords were permitted to speak. David Perez then asked whether the thirteen who had been arrested three weeks before and were now out on bail could be invited. Under the terms of their bail agreement, they were forced to stay one hundred yards from the church unless the officials of the church specifically asked them to come in. A church spokesman extended a reluctant invitation. Within minutes the group arrived, led by Felipe Luciano, his broken arm dangling in its cast under a khaki military jacket. He moved up the aisle and began talking. His Spanish is poor, and he made his address in English, while Perez handled the simultaneous translation. Luciano is small and compact, with a large afro. His manner is self-possessed. Before he started talking, one elderly believer seemed to faint and she was helped outside by five people, two of them Lords. Another woman went to her knees and began sobbing loudly, calling upon God to save her church and drive these devils out. But within minutes the entire chapel was hushed, and only Luciano's words, followed by their Spanish equivalents, could be heard.

He began with a recapitulation of the conflict and proceeded quickly to social perceptions, which had been nurtured in jail and on the street, being given impetus and direction by Cleaver, Malcolm, Che, and Pedro Albizu-Campos. Our children are kept hungry, he said, not just with no food, but with no understanding of who they are. Their culture is being driven out of them. Their true social aspirations are being denied. But still, despite these attempts, there is a residual bond, a communal life that must be given greater expression. The people of the barrio don't have to be taught socialism, they have been living it all their lives. But the agencies that supposedly are to tend to their welfare are not doing their job. The Church talks about honoring God, but how can that be done without honoring man? Without feeding children and without providing for life? With his eyes searing and searching, he went on extemporaneously talking of coming together, of a solidarity of the soul and a union of commitment. Then he said he would like to end by reciting one of his poems.

Michael T. Kaufman

And with a voice that rolled in and around the words, he whammed it in to them, Lords and pietists alike.

Jíbaro
mi negro lindo
del bosque de cana
do los cariques de luz
Tiempo es una cosa cómica

Jíbaro
my pretty nigger
The earth of my people
Father of the sweet smells of fruit
    in my mother's womb
The earth brown of my skin
The thoughts of freedom
that butterfly through my insides

Jíbaro
my pretty nigger
Sweating bullets of blood and bedbugs
Swaying slowly to a softly strummed
five-string guitar
Remembering ancient empires of
Sun Gods and Black Spirits
and things that were once so simple

How times have changed men
How men have changed times
"Unnatural," screams the wind, "unnatural."

Jíbaro
my pretty nigger man
Fish smells and
    cane smells and fish smells and
    cane smells and tobacco

And oppression makes even God smell foul
As foul as the bowels of the ship
That vomited you on the harbors of a cold,
        metal city
To die
No sun   no sand   no palm trees
And you clung to the slimy ribs of the animal called
the marine tiger
In the name of the Father, the Son and
        the Holy Ghost, Amen.

Jíbaro
did you know my nigger?
I love the curve of your brow
the slant of your babies' eyes
the calves of your women dancing
I dig you
You can't hide
I ride with you on subways
touch shoulders with you in dances
Make crazy love to your daughter

Yeah
You my cold nigger man
And I love you 'cause you mine
And I'll never let you go
And I'll never let you go (you mine, nigger)
And I'll never let you go (forget about self,
        we together now)
And I'll never let you go.

It was the most religious thing that had happened in the
church in the last eight weeks. And for a few minutes, as
the ark emptied, it appeared that there were no differences
between the Lords and the parishioners. Only the whites

who had come in support might have felt alien. Some of them seemed to want to be somebody's pretty nigger.

By the following Sunday, however, any vision of compromise dissolved. During the week, the Lords strengthened the language of their demands. The free breakfasts were not negotiable: all the church could do was to accept them. There was somewhat more latitude on the liberation school. The church people were in an impossible situation. They could not call the police in since that, obviously, would only strengthen their adversaries. They could not give in since they felt that would mean ceding autonomy. They could have sought the intercession of liberal church groups, but this tack, when attempted, fell apart because the interfaith council itself was split over the Lords' demands. Clearly the Lords were attacking and the church was defending. And clearly, too, the church had no place to retreat to, except to the street. That is where they went the week after Felipe read his poem. Services ended and the Lords again got up to speak. The minister led the faithful out, paying no attention to the talk. And when the parishioners had left, wham, bang, bang, the double doors of the church were bolted shut from the inside. Large wooden crosspieces were nailed to the doors. A portable bullhorn, that indispensable tool of all street organizations, was put through an office window, and a young woman kept repeating in Spanish and English that the church now belonged to the people. As the congregation gathered on the street outside to sing its hymns, the blare of the amplifier drowned out the lilt of the carols. "This is your church, Iglesia de Pueblo." Luciano and Yoruba, both forbidden from entering the church under the terms of an injunction that the church had obtained, watched and listened from across the street.

Meanwhile, the machinery was set in motion. A bust

might come at any time. Bodies would be needed. The word went out, and during that Sunday students from all over the city came down. A group of Puerto Rican leaders expressed qualified support for the Lords. A contingent from the Bronx representing an amalgam of Hispanic groups demonstrated their support. Lords functionaries worked to set up the breakfast program and liberation school. Food was collected from neighborhood merchants. Some said it was extorted, but Luciano explained that no one was threatened. "These merchants have charged high prices and lived off these people for a long time. They know there have been riots in East Harlem, so when they give us stuff, that's not a matter of extortion. It's just smart business." A few Lords with a knowledge of plumbing got the church's heating plant working. Others were assigned to a security detail at the door. Anyone entering the church had to submit to a thorough search. Women searched the women, and men searched the men. Anything resembling a weapon—penknifes, nail files, hatpins—was confiscated, marked with the name of the owner, and set aside. Within two days there were about a hundred youngsters coming each morning for breakfast. Many of the younger ones spent the entire day in classrooms, where they drew flags of Puerto Rico, played, and listened to music and stories. A loudspeaker system was hooked up to a phonograph downstairs, and all day long, records and tapes were played. The voices of Martin Luther King, Malcolm X, and Cleaver carried through the hall, where small discussion groups were being held. In between the speeches there was record music like "Mighty, Mighty, Spade and Whitey." Among the visitors who came from downtown to put in some hours with the Lords were Elia Kazan, the writer and director, and Budd Schulberg, the novelist. They had come with their friend José Torres, a former light heavyweight champion, who is sometimes thought of as a potential political leader for New York's Puerto Ricans. "This is beautiful," said Schulberg after touring the pulsating complex.

Earlier that morning Juan Gonzalez had lectured to the social studies classes of the Manhattan Day School, a progressive biracial private school. As the sixty fourth- and fifth-grade youngsters sat attentively in camp chairs, Gonzalez explained, "The people from the church believe that the problems people have now can be solved in heaven. If you're hungry now, you'll get fed in heaven. If you're cold, you'll get a set of wings and a decent place to live in heaven. We don't believe that. Our religion is that we have to get these things for each other here and now. That's why we say that we serve the people." A little girl raised her hand and asked why the church people were so afraid of the Lords. "Well," answered Gonzalez, "they see the way we are dressed and our long hair and they think we read and talk about people who they are afraid of. They call us devils. But we are not afraid of them. If they let us have part of the church for the breakfast program, we would not prevent them from holding their services or singing their songs, although we ourselves probably would not take part." The children were asked if they wanted to buy Lords buttons for five cents, and most said they did. Then Gonzalez asked which of them had lost a set of braces.

Throughout the eleven days of activity, the threat of a bust, real or imagined, hovered over the group. There were several false alarms when the Lords expected, or at least said they expected, the police to come. Telephone calls were made and reinforcements recruited, not necessarily to battle with the police but to show the magnitude of support. On the Feast of the Epiphany, a big Puerto Rican holiday, a party was planned with singing and dancing late into the night. For a while it appeared that the police would come then, but the party proceeded without interruptions. While in the church these flurries of tension erupted periodically, at the office, where legal work was being coordinated, all was smooth. The church had obtained an injunction prohibiting the Lords from interfering with the regular observances in the building. Since this was a civil injunction, it was handled by the sheriff's office. The Lords' lawyers arranged for the sheriff to come to the door of the church. They handed his deputy a bullhorn and stood by as he vocally served the citation. The order to vacate was, of course, ignored, and the lawyers for the church went back to court to seek a contempt citation. The young lawyers for the Lords marshaled a slew of arguments, all centered around what a church is supposed to be. Is it merely a corporation, an economic entity, or does it have a mission and a separate identity? For the time being, these arguments were set aside, and the youths occupying the church were cited with civil contempt. An arrest order was signed and turned over to the sheriff. He could have sought the help of the police in exercising it, but the Lords' lawyers persuaded him to negotiate the terms of the arrest. Even as the inside of the church buzzed with fears of an impending bust, and medical supplies were brought in by teams of volunteer doctors and nurses, the lawyers were drawing up an agreement. The sheriff and his men would come between six and seven in the morning. He would have to break down the door, but the people inside the church would offer no resistance and would come out into waiting police vans. The sheriff was skeptical, but finally he agreed.

The night before the arrests was a busy one inside the church. Food, toys, and clothing were collected and removed. Crews set about cleaning the place. Teams of lawyers interviewed each person who wanted to stay. If anyone had a case pending on some other legal action, he was advised to leave. Information for bail was collected and taken out of the building. Then in the wintry darkness, as dawn crept up from Queens, the trucks began arriving. About one thousand blue-helmeted policemen took up positions all around the neighborhood. Traffic was sealed off from the major thoroughfares. There were cops on the roofs of most of the buildings. Twelve paddy wagons stood parked around the corner. Inside the church the people were gathering their sleeping bags and books. The sheriff had a policeman batter down the door. And then he read the arrest order.

It was just as the lawyers had said it would be. The first group of twenty came out, fists held high and shouting, "Power to the people," and then they and many of those inside began singing, "Que bonita bandera, que bonita bandera, que bonita bandera es la bandera puertorriqueña." ("Oh, what a beautiful flag is the flag of Puerto Rico.") The police stood around. There was nothing for them to do. The siege of the First Spanish Methodist Church had ended. The last of the 105 squatters were carried off to court, where they were released on their own recognizance for a later hearing on the contempt citation. All that remained of the occupation was a sign saying "The People's Church" stuck in a window.

A coda: the flush of fervor dwindled as the romantic and quixotic cadre became a force. Gonzalez's prediction came true. Dogma mounted and humanism ebbed. The breakfast program dwindled and disappeared. The search for lead paint stopped. And Felipe Luciano, who raised consciousness so well, was purged for the romantic, bourgeois, *macho* crime of male chauvinism. Apparently his poetic sensibilities attracted to him chicks of many races, creeds, and national origins. He was busted back to cadre rank and stuck it out for a while, appearing at demonstrations like a soldier. Then he left for a career as a writer and a teacher of poetry. The other Lords, meanwhile, began concentrating more and more on Puerto Rico and not New York. Yoruba got convicted for draft evasion, but while he was on bail he visited Peking. He came back. The struggle now, say the Lords, is not merely to improve life under oppressive conditions, but to break the shackles tying Puerto Rico to the mother country.

Can a Girl from a Small Town in Arkansas Find Fame and Happiness by Floating over Central Park on Balloons, Playing Her Cello?

It was a cool September evening, and an eleven-year-old black boy named Buddy had been playing hide-and-seek in the wooded hills of Central Park at its northern end, where it abuts Harlem, where white people don't go. Buddy, who was the seeker, heard voices and tinkly music coming through the trees and started to find out where the sound was coming from, leaving the hiders. He cut through the weedy bramble and climbed a rock, and there before him on the roadway that runs through the park were fifteen flatbed trucks with flashing lights and neon sculptures. A jazz band was playing down the road. A man was walking on fifteen-foot stilts. Another man was filling large balloons with helium gas. Most of the people rushing around were white, but some were green and orange and some were painted in many colors. One woman was dressed in an elaborate wedding gown. With her was a groom in evening clothes, with a ceremonial sash and medals over his boiled white shirt. He also wore a gas mask. Buddy stood on his bluff and whistled: "Shit!" A man in a harlequin outfit who was giving out long-stemmed daffodils to the children who were flocking around the floats saw Buddy and told him to come down. "Look," said the man, who was Japanese, "I need you to hit these tin cans with sticks when the parade starts." Buddy picked up a stick and the man showed him and some other children how they were to go about hitting the squashed cans during the two-mile parade. "When are we going to start?" asked Buddy. And the man answered that he didn't know, that they should have moved out an hour ago but that something seemed to be holding things up. None of the kids seemed to mind the delay. They jumped from one float to another, dancing in front of the flashing strobe lights that made them move like animated stick figures. But way back at the end of the parade formation a very serious discussion was taking place about the delay. A tall thin man in a dark suit and porkpie hat, looking as out of place as a missionary at a cannibal soiree, was talking to a plump young woman in a black evening gown.

"Look, that woman is going to take her clothes off and she has a Vietcong flag," said the man, who worked for the public relations department of Consolidated Edison. "Don't be silly," said the woman in black, who was Charlotte Moorman, the impresario of the avant-garde. "Of course she is not going to take her clothes off." "Look," said the Con Edison man, "we gave you the trucks for the floats on the condition that there would be no nudity and no heavy politics, right? And now that woman is going to take her clothes off and march with a Vietcong flag. We can't start the parade if she does that."

Miss Moorman, who has been staging festivals of the avant-garde every year since 1961, refused to be ruffled. Even when reporters approached and asked what was holding things up, she smiled and explained that everything was normal, that she had been late to her own wedding and that no one could expect artists, least of all artists who walk on stilts and play with electronic devices, to be on time for anything. Smiling, she asked the reporters, "Isn't all this beautiful?" and she gestured to the darkening park road ahum with generators and flashing like a firefly convention.

Having parried the press, she turned back to the Con Edison man. She told him she would confer with the suspect woman. While the Con Edison man stood a few feet away and watched, Miss Moorman told the woman that she hoped she wouldn't take her clothes off and walk naked with other members of her troupe under an unfurled Vietcong flag. In her soft southwestern drawl she explained that this would jeopardize the whole parade and the future of the annual festival. She explained that hundreds of people had spent thousands of their own dollars on their exhibits, and that if people took their clothes off Con Edison would take their trucks back. It was hard for Miss Moorman to say all this. Particularly since she herself has taken her clothes off during cello recitals on two continents. She understands the limitlessness of the artistic imagination, but she understood, too, that there simply wasn't enough time to expand the consciousness and artistic awareness of Con Edison, and she had no doubt that if anyone took their clothes off there would be no parade. The lady of the flag, at that moment decorously attired, listened to all this sullenly. She had in the past moved to many areas of the city, disrobed stealthily with her troupe and paraded and danced nude, sometimes with a Vietcong flag and sometimes without. That was what the lady did. It was her response to the world around her, and she'd be damned if a public utility would circumscribe her freedom. Miss Moorman, who had weathered greater obstacles, tried again to explain the realities, but was interrupted this time by one of the Vietcong lady's male troupe members, who punched her in the stomach. The Con Edison man saw that and realized that Miss Moorman was obviously sincere in trying to honor her commitment to no nakedness and no heavy politics. He moved in with some brawny utility workers. Somehow they and Miss Moorman banished the Vietcong lady and her followers. A whistle blew, the order was shouted to move on, and the parade took off.

The bride and groom took up the lead, followed by the stilt-walker, followed by hundreds of kids, including Buddy, who was whacking hell out of an old beer can. There was another contingent of kids who rolled giant oil cans, painted yellow, blue, and red, down the march route. On the trucks, music blared and fluorescent light sculptures fluoresced. Joe Jones rode a tricycle he had built that had a tall metal superstructure in the back on which there was a violin in a birdcage and some drums and concertinas. When he rode, little battery-operated motors activated the instruments, creating random music that varied with the contours of the road. It was sensational until an overhanging tree branch did Mr. Jones in, overturning his machine and dazing the artist. Later that night he went to the emergency ward of a hospital for treatment. The intern asked him how he got the scrapes, and Joe Jones, who is a thirty-seven-year-old former monk, said he had fallen off his tricycle.

Meanwhile, other small catastrophes were happening. Jim McWilliams, who used to be a professor of graphic design, was blowing up eight large balloons with helium. Helium is expensive. All together it cost him $1,000. He was blowing up the balloons so that Charlotte could be attached to them by a harness and play her cello suspended over the heads of the paraders. After all, if Macy's could float Donald Duck every Thanksgiving, why not? But while Mr. McWilliams was filling up the balloons, some kid, or, as Mr. McWilliams called him, "some little disturbed bastard," popped one of the balloons with his stick, freeing $150 worth of helium. The remaining balloons had barely enough lift to hoist Charlotte's 130 pounds and cello. With McWilliams holding a tether line, Charlotte bobbed some fifteen feet above the heads of the marchers and spectators, stroking her cello to make music. Downdrafts sent her plummeting and dipping, but in seconds she'd be up again.

The parade wound through the park, out onto the street, and then down to Columbus Circle. By midnight the Con Edison people had dismantled the trucks, and people started to go home or to parties. The year's Festival of the Avant-Garde had ended. Buddy, who stayed with the parade all the way, thought it was fantastic. A fat lady at Eighty-sixth Street said she thought "it was a big nothing." The artist participants thought it was marvelous and they all came to hug and kiss Charlotte, whom they all recognize as the protective mother for a group of people that, for want of a better word, are called avant-garde.

Charlotte wants a better word but hasn't found one. *Avant-garde*, she says, means ahead of our time, "but how can things that are actually done be ahead of our time? Once they are done, they are of our time." Anyway, Charlotte has this telephone book with about seven thousand names and numbers, and in that book are just about all the artists that belong to this movement as well as collectors and benefactors and critics and cab drivers and other people whom she likes and who like her. But the artists in that book are very difficult to categorize. Some make sounds and some make images. Some, like Christo, a Bulgarian, do incredibly big things like wrapping a two-mile stretch of the coast of Australia. Some, like Eric Segal, work with incredibly complex television technology, making electronic images and patterns. There are several loose common denominators that more or less apply to most of these people. For one thing, they seem to be moving away from galleries and concert halls. They resent their art, which is their life, being weighed and justified by objects that someone can hang on a wall. For many of them art is much more of a verb than it is a noun. Then, too, most of them perceive in terms of very contemporary symbols. They have understood that the commonplace magic of television sets and videotapes and electronics has replaced, or at least augmented, the commonplace magic of cows and trees and is, therefore, suitable grist for artistic and aesthetic exploration. Another common thread is the seriousness of those involved. Certainly there is a strong element of humor, but there is also a terribly strong commitment that manifests itself in self-sacrifice in terms of dollars and flesh that these people expend on their art. A man like McWilliams will spend thousands of dollars of his own money creating things that can never be sold, that are by their nature ephemeral. But he does it, he says, because the feeling he has when his things are done well "is better than food, better than sex, better than anything."

Finally, what they have in common is Charlotte, and through her and her festivals and her notebook they have each other. She has been called the Jeanne d'Arc of the new art, and while she has yet to be burned at the stake she has been jailed and vilified by the establishment critics. Through it all she has maintained an innocence that those who know her only superficially often think of as put on. It is not. She is a country girl in a big city who disarms the powerful with her sincerity and her obvious devotion to her art and her artists. Just as she maneuvered Con Edison into giving her trucks and generators, so she has beguiled mayors and commissioners, without money and without political influence. Once she got a New York City ferryboat for a twenty-four-hour festival, and as the vessel made its normal crossings from Staten Island to Manhattan, picking up and discharging regular passengers, her artists showed their works and themselves. Other times it was an island in the East River, an armory, and once most of Central Park. There were always obstacles, lawsuits, and threats of lawsuits. There was never any money, except for that shelled out by the artists themselves. And now, when Charlotte has gotten a good deal of recognition, mostly in Europe, as a creative artist, and after she has played as an invited guest at the prestigious Venice Biennale, she still devotes herself for months on end to her festival, to present a forum where the very living art of her friends can be seen, heard, and felt.

How she came to be impresario of all this is, to Charlotte, the most natural thing in the world. But then again Charlotte concedes that she views things a little differently than do other people. There she was, a girl who learned her Bach and Brahms growing up around Little Rock. Going to Centenary College in Shreveport. Getting her master's degree in cello at the University of Texas. Getting a scholarship to Meadowmount camp for music and studying with Leonard Rose. Playing Bach and Brahms. Marrying her college sweetheart, a double bass player. Then he got a job with the Buffalo Philharmonic and they went to Buffalo and, well, she really felt different there and people had trouble understanding her, so after a summer in Buffalo she left the double bass player, who she says was a wonderful man, and came to New York and went to

Juilliard. And played Bach and Brahms. She lived with three other women students and practiced four, five hours a day, and because she had no money she ate pizzas and Cokes and hot dogs, and just a while ago she paid for that by having her gall bladder removed. But it was great and interesting. All except the Kabalevsky cello concerto. She had played it thirty-five times in school recitals. Now, as she was ending her studies at Juilliard, there it was facing her again. It was too much. She went around looking for something else to play and she found a piece by John Cage. It was called "26 Minutes, 1.499 Seconds for a String Player." The notation was completely different. There were places in it where the composer left room for the musician to make different kinds of noises. It was a fascinating thing, but her teachers wouldn't let her do it. So she did the Kabalevsky for the thirty-sixth time, but something had changed. She left Juilliard and became an eminently respectable cellist. She was playing under Leopold Stokowski with the New American Symphony and getting studio jobs and advertising work and beginning to make it. She still supplemented her income by working at a phone answering agency, but a lot less.

Then one day she met Kenjii Kabayashi, a Japanese pianist who had been a classmate at Juilliard, and he told her he was going back to Japan. Charlotte asked him how could he go back without having a Town Hall concert, and he said he couldn't have a concert because he didn't have the $1,000 for the rental of the hall. Charlotte says that Kenjii was a genius. Charlotte also says that most of her artist friends are geniuses. This does not, of course, mean that they are not. Charlotte says she has never understood money, and maybe for that reason she could not understand why Kenjii had to forgo his concert. Having made up her mind that this was stupid, she set about raising money for the concert. There is a large Japanese artistic community in New York, and Charlotte, who at that time did not know any of its members, tracked down people like Isamu Noguchi, the sculptor, and told them that their countryman Kenjii, who was a genius, was going home without his recital and that this was a crime, so would they please give her a thousand dollars to rent the hall. Noguchi said he'd give $100 if nine other people or organizations like the Japanese Chamber of Commerce would give a similar contribution. In five days Charlotte had the money. She rented the hall and made contact with an adventurous impresario named Norman Seaman, who, at no cost and some loss to himself, presented Kenjii's concert. One of the things he played at that concert was a piece by a modern Japanese composer named Toshi Ichiyanagi, who was then leaving New York and divorcing his wife. The wife was a sculptor-poet-singer-actress-artist, who was the daughter of a wealthy Japanese banking family. Her name was Yoko Ono, and she became Charlotte's roommate in a very bourgeois apartment house on West End Avenue.

By this time, which was in 1961, Charlotte was still playing Bach and Brahms and working with the New American Symphony, but she was also working on her own with the Cage piece her Juilliard teachers wouldn't let her play. One day Yoko told Charlotte that she was ready to give a concert-recital-performance and asked Charlotte to arrange it for her. Charlotte said she didn't know how, but Yoko remembered what she had done for Kenjii, and Charlotte, again with Mr. Seaman, worked it out. That performance marked the world premiere of Yoko's "cut piece," in which members of the audience are invited to cut and shred the costume of individual performers. Since then Charlotte has done "cut piece" hundreds of times all over the world and, unlike the Kabalevsky, it has been different every time and she is not sick of it. She plays and the audience snips. After every performance she sends her torn garments to a Yoko Ono fan in Germany who collects them as souvenirs.

From Yoko's concert to the Festival of the Avant-Garde was a simple and direct transition. Charlotte had met Cage and Edgard Varèse and Earle Brown, the trio of adventurous serious musical innovators, who were each individually exploring new forms of sounds and silences. She was playing regularly in downtown lofts with people excited by these new forms. One was a pianist named Frederic Rzewski, who had just come back from two years in Europe, where, as a Fulbright student, he had met with some success in concerts. He sometimes played with gloves on, and Charlotte remembers that he did brilliant, incredible things. Rzewski, who is now a music director for a Brooklyn church and still does incredible things on the side, was having trouble getting concerts here. Charlotte took his case to Norman Seaman, whom she wore down and who agreed to sponsor a concert at Judson Hall, across the street from Carnegie Hall. Somehow, by the time Charlotte got through with the planning, that concert had grown to a four-night festival of the new music. It was held in August of 1962 and was the first Festival of the Avant-Garde. Charlotte got Varèse and Cage and Brown to contribute pieces, and she got all sorts of people to perform. No one got paid, and admissions were cheap, covering the rental of the hall, or almost covering it, and Mr. Seaman made up the rest. Charlotte remembers that event as being wonderful. The critics were less kind, but Charlotte bears them no malice. They just don't understand, the poor people, she says. Generally and collectively she regards critics, or at least American critics, as "the oldest young people" she knows.

A similar mostly music festival was presented by Charlotte in 1963. The big breakthrough, however, into intermedia and into notoriety came the following year with the third festival. Again, Charlotte started rounding up her troupe and getting pieces. With her flamboyant innocence, she marched in on the grand and the famous and in simple terms told them what she wanted. It is hard to turn her down. One of the people she went to see was Karlheinz Stockhausen, the iconoclastic German composer, whom she asked for a piece for her festival. Stockhausen at first told her he had nothing that could be done by anything less than a symphony orchestra. Well, asked Charlotte, not too put off by anything less than a declaration of war, couldn't he write something? Stockhausen thought awhile and recalled that, yes, there was something he had that maybe could be done. It was a theater piece called *Originale* and it ran ninety-four minutes. But he thought again and said it couldn't be done. Why? asked Charlotte. Well, said Stockhausen, the piece, which had been commissioned and performed in Cologne, needed a painter who'd do action painting. Charlotte said she could get a painter. And, said Stockhausen, it needed two lighting men. No problem, said Charlotte. And it needed four models who dress and undress, and a mother, and two children, and a director, and fourteen percussionists and a string player and six actors and a hatcheck girl, and some film, and a poet and a pianist and a conductor. Also it needed a chimpanzee. Charlotte said she could get all that. Stockhausen then said the piece also needed Nam June Paik, that all the other participants simply had to be themselves for set periods of time while Stockhausen's electronic music piece

Kontakte was played. He explained that any model could be herself, but no one could be Nam June Paik but Nam June Paik, and Nam June Paik was in Germany, so that was that and she could not have the piece. Charlotte asked Stockhausen what the hell a Nam June Paik was, and he told her that he was a Korean who had worked in Germany for the last eight years, that he was a genius, a pianist, and an electronic wizard. Charlotte said that if he was that important she would write him in Germany and get him to come. Stockhausen said that if Paik came, she could do the piece. Charlotte went home to her rooms in an uptown residential hotel where she had begun living since Yoko went back to Japan. She had been home for an hour when the phone rang. "Moo-man, here is Paik," said the voice at the other end. "Stockhausen tell me you want me. We do *Originale*. We be partners. We meet." Charlotte asked him when he could get to the United States, and Paik explained that he was in the United States, and had been here for exactly an hour. He said he would meet her in the next hour so they could plan their partnership, which he indicated was to go far beyond *Originale*. Charlotte met him at a luncheonette not far from where she worked answering phones. She recalls that the first thing the slight, unsmiling Korean said to her was, "Okay, we do *Originale* no problem. I have robot. Robot walk in front of performance. He very good bisexual robot. He walk, talk, and shit white beans. Then you me be partners. You play Saint-Saëns. You play half. Then you stop and dive into water like swan, then you get out and finish playing. You wear only pee-jama." It turned out that what Paik referred to as a pee-jama was a nightgown made of transparent plastic, but Charlotte didn't get to know that until later, and that, she says, was just as well.

On September 8, Paik's robot paraded in front of Jud-

son Hall along with pickets carrying signs that said "Don't
let Stockhausen tell you Folk Art is Primitive," and "Fight
the Art of the Social Climbers." The robot just kept repeating, "Don't ask what your country can do for you, but
what you can do for your country." Then the pickets put
down their signs and went in to take part in the performance of the American premiere of *Originale* as directed by
the creator of the happening, Allen Kaprow, with Allen
Ginsberg playing the poet, Priscilla the chimpanzee being
herself, Charlotte Moorman and her cello, and Nam June
Paik performing as Nam June Paik. Things went off pretty
much as unplanned, although the various participants
came on and off the stage for their bits with precision,
being themselves for exactly the right number of minutes
and seconds. Ginsberg recited a poem and giggled. Children built castles with blocks. Apples were thrown. Someone delivered a monologue in Greek. Somebody else
dropped eggs and spices onto a sheet from a ladder,
making either an action painting or an omelet. Charlotte
played her cello while sitting on a rail in the balcony of the
concert hall, and Paik was just magnificent. He squirted
himself with shaving cream all over. Then he sprinkled
himself with rice, and then he entered into a trough of
water, drinking from his own shoe. He cut off somebody's
tie. Then two men came out from the audience. Paik cut
off the tie of one of the men with a scissors. The other man
took out a pair of handcuffs and attached Paik to a
scaffold, which was the dominant part of the set. Paik
screamed that he could not get out. It was inspired. The
audience thought it was great, or at least some of the audience did. Charlotte thought it was dreadful because the
part about the handcuffs was not in the script. Paik was really handcuffed, a prisoner on stage. Not only that, but his
allotted time for being himself was almost over. Charlotte

then did a very foolish thing. She called the police, reporting that a man was handcuffed to a scaffold at a concert hall and would they please send help. No sooner had she made the call when she spotted Mr. Seaman, who was also aware of Paik's distress. He told Charlotte that he would call a locksmith, but that whatever they did he just wanted to make sure that no one called the police, explaining that just about everything that was happening in the performance violated some regulation. The models were about to disrobe. Though a trainer had been obtained for the chimp, Priscilla had a way of escaping from him. The children were underage. There were fire hazards. Things like that. "Oh, my God," shouted Charlotte, and ran to call the police again, saying that there was no one handcuffed at the theater. But this call was to no avail, for within minutes six patrolmen from the emergency division arrived to free Paik, who was still railing at the railing. The performance went on, and many in the audience thought the cops were supposed to be there. They freed Paik and were being thanked and ushered out just as the first model arrived and started to disrobe. The police stood around and watched. Mr. Seaman stood with them, chatting amiably. From the wings the other performers watched the scene at the back of the concert hall. It was very tense. But then, as the model shed one outfit and was getting into another, the police shrugged, smiled, and left. Not all police are philistines.

Through her involvement with people like Paik and Kaprow, Charlotte's notebook began to grow. In addition to musicians, there were now poets, painters, sculptors, electricians. She was still working primarily as a traditional cellist, but more and more she was appearing with Paik at small gatherings. She and the Korean genius had enacted his vision of the Saint-Saëns variations in pee-jama. Once, when they did it in Philadelphia, she suffered a three-inch gash on her cheek when she dove into the tank of water, but with blood streaming on her transparent nightgown she got out and finished the piece. That summer she and Paik hired a gondola and she did the piece diving into the Grand Canal in Venice at the appropriate time. She was sick for weeks after, and she says she is the only person in the world who did not know the canal is polluted. That performance coincided with the Biennale, the festival of creative art held every two years in the Italian city. Charlotte and Paik, who understand the uses of publicity, were in a sense crashing the festival. Six years later Charlotte was officially invited to perform at the Biennale, which made her very proud.

The festival in 1965 was significant in two ways: for one thing, Mr. Seaman bowed out of the sponsorship, leaving it all to Charlotte, who is very understanding of his disengagement. She thinks that Mr. Seaman was angelic to put up with her artists for as long as he did. There were suits after every festival. The piano people complained that artists had strewn flowers in the instrument's innards, and things like that. The egos of the artists were often as fragile as the financial arrangements for the recitals. Mr. Seaman was losing money and sleep. So, without money and still subsisting largely on hot dogs and bologna sandwiches, Charlotte undertook the responsibilities of management.

The other significant thing about the 1965 festival, Charlotte's first solo attempt, was that it was the last at Judson. Because of police intervention the management of the hall indicated there would be no more festivals there. This last one, to run for thirteen days, included a film night and an evening of jazz, as well as several concerts of music by Cage, Brown, and Satie. Tickets, which sold for ninety-nine cents, were the prime source of financing. The artists, as before, volunteered their performances. Everything was going smoothly, with the little hall filled to its 300-seat capacity every night. Until the ninth night. That was when Allen Kaprow did his "push-pull" piece that had been commissioned by The Museum of Modern Art. There was some music in the first part of the program, and then at intermission Mr. Kaprow enlisted the audience for his piece. On the stage he erected flats enclosing two rooms, a living room and an attic. The audience, he explained, would have twenty minutes during the intermission to go out into the street and scavenge furniture or things that could go into either of the rooms. The next thing that happened was that 300 well-dressed men and women, some of them quite distinguished, fanned out from West Fifty-seventh Street in an area of hotels and tourists, poring through refuse and garbage cans. Some found old tires and broken TV sets and gooseneck lamps. Officers in cruising police cars observed the phenomenon. Some of them followed the parade of people and bric-a-brac back to the concert hall and made inquiries. Some of these inquiries involved waking up the manager of the hall and having him come in from New Jersey. The explanations that were finally accepted by the police did not disrupt the outfitting of the two rooms. But the incident did antagonize the management to the point where they threatened to cancel the remaining nights. They ultimately recanted on the threat, but the whole thing raised Charlotte's resolve to move the festival to places where ordinary people would have a chance to see this new art.

So, almost immediately after the '65 festival had ended, the Jeanne d'Arc of the avant-garde asked the city fathers to give her Central Park for a full twenty-four-hour day of creativity. The commissioner of parks at the time was Thomas P. F. Hoving, who had been curator at the Metropolitan Museum. He was then eagerly encouraging wider use of city parkland, and maybe because of this concern he succumbed to the single-minded innocence of Miss Moorman, giving her the park on September 9, 1966. In the interim artists from all over the United States were writing and calling Charlotte, volunteering to perform. In a realm where standards are regarded as ridiculous and where symbolism is generally left to the beholder, it is very difficult to be selective. Essentially Charlotte solved this problem by encouraging almost everyone. Sincerity and devotion to whatever one does seem to be the qualifications she looks for.

Take the case of Jim McWilliams. Jim is now a thirty-seven-year-old art director for the New York Port Authority, but back in '66 he was a tenured professor and head of the graphic arts department at the Philadelphia College of Art, an acknowledged expert on typefaces, printing, and printmaking. But a few years before that he had started moving off in a new direction, and except for his students there were not too many people in Philadelphia who could understand. For instance, there was the time he invited his class to paint his new Dodge convertible, thus depreciating its value by $800 in two hours. There was the time he and a number of students shaved their heads by degrees, going bald within a week, in a sort of experiment in gradual change. Once he hired eight yellow taxicabs, giving them precise choreographic instruction as to where to turn, where to open a door, and where to turn on their lights. He called the exercise "Dance for Yellow Taxicabs." Once he gave his class an assignment to work up something, either in time or space, involving progressions from one to twenty. One of his better students fulfilled the assignment by challenging his teacher to drink twenty consecutive shots of scotch. Being a conscientious teacher, he tried, but, with the whole class watching, he collapsed in a stupor at sixteen. The faculty looked askance at all this, but they recognized that Jim was a good teacher and that the students liked him, and he would still be there if he hadn't recognized that Philadelphia is surrounded "by a gigantic plastic dome that has been there since Revolutionary times."

Even while working at the school, he would frequently drive his psychedelic depreciated car to New York several times a week. He had met Charlotte when she and Paik had played a concert at the school, and had been overwhelmed. Since that time he and she had done things on the same programs in lofts and Greenwich Village theaters and churches. So, when the park festival was planned, Charlotte called Jim and invited him to participate. Several weeks before the festival, she called again to ask what he would be doing.

"I thought a picnic would be nice," said Jim.

"A picnic? Fabulous. Of course, what would be better in the park than a picnic?" said Charlotte.

"Yep, I'll come down with hot dogs and watermelon and soda and everybody will eat themselves sick."

"Oh, that's great," said Charlotte.

But what she didn't realize just then was that McWilliams meant exactly what he said. He had been thinking of an event—he calls them episodes—suitable for the park. Then he got a flash. Picnics. They are American; they are also an established artistic theme. So, at the appointed time, Jim drove a van onto a grassy meadow. A few hundred yards away, two jazz trumpeters were echoing each other across a pond, and off in another direction Alison Knowles was inviting people to come to a microphone to tell the story of their shoes. A young man, one of the dozens who accepted the invitation, said, "These shoes I am wearing are not sneakers. They are athletic shoes and most of the greatest basketball players wear them. And I am a credit to them. Thank you very much."

Jim turned on a tape playing rock music in his van. He brought out boxes and boxes of frankfurters and started cooking them on grills he had set up. He had obtained the necessary fire permit. People came by and he gave them hot dogs and soda. He ate hot dogs himself. Many hot dogs. Ten, twelve hot dogs. Most of the people just ate one hot dog, but some were getting into the spirit of the thing as much as Jim was and ate lots. Jim was the first to vomit. But that did not slow him down. He kept eating. Then somebody else vomited. It was a regular epidemic. People vomiting all around. The smell of the burning hot dogs mixed with the nauseating cud on the grass. Some Parks Department people grew alarmed and attempted to stop the spectacle, but couldn't get close enough past the foul odor to express themselves. Naturally, some people drifted away, refusing the proffered hot dogs, but Jim kept on eating. He kept on throwing up, too. A few who seemed to understand joined him. But pretty soon it was over. Jim then set about cleaning up the mess, which he always does at his episodes. There were many who found the whole thing disgusting, but some understood. Said one young visitor to his girl friend, "It really makes sense. Hot dogs are American. Picnics are American, and what the hell is more American than gluttony? Where else do people eat themselves sick?"

Other artists thought Jim's episode was very strong, very direct. Generally, when these other artists talk about Jim, they get around to his stamina, they say that when he does something he never does it by half measures. There was the time, for instance, when he had moved to New York and took a job as professor of graphic design at Cooper

Union. He was living in a loft on Walker Street, a narrow thoroughfare in SoHo, which has become the residential art center of the Western world. At that time Jim belonged to a loose confederation of artists who presented shows in their homes and lofts. These shows would go on for a few hours on specified days. Jim got an idea for a two-week show that would go on day and night. It was called "Views of Walker Street." Jim went to the company that makes those telescopes that you put a dime in so you can then scan panoramas from places like the Empire State Building. He conned them into lending him six such machines. He then placed the viewers at each of his six windows, inviting people to come up anytime to look, either outward or, pivoting the things around, back into the depths of his home. But his most heroic exploit, according to his artist friends, was the crawling piece he devised for the festival that Charlotte held on the ferryboat. He arrived in a rubber frogman's suit with diving mask, and for a full twenty-four hours, with no breaks for food or coffee, he crawled slowly all over the vessel. "I was a little disappointed that some of the other artists just did their things when the press was there," said Jim. "They really wasted an opportunity to get into a different time scan. It's not what the public missed, but what they denied themselves. About the sixteenth hour of my crawl, I really went into something. It was unbelievable, you really become and feel different." Jim says that for him and his art "the audience is just a leftover tradition." He had never made anything in recent years that could possibly be sold, although he used to make and still could make merchandisable prints. In fact, almost everything he makes costs him in either "flesh or dollars." His exhibit at Charlotte's 1971 festival, a gigantic nine-foot-high birthday cake out of which Charlotte emerged, cost $800 and has not yet been fully paid for.

Michael T. Kaufman

Most of the people in Charlotte's book are like that. They are all artists, none are dilettantes. They live their art, and if that means subsidizing it out of pocket and flesh, well, so be it. Perhaps the most successful of the creators is Christo, the Bulgarian who is referred to time and again by his contemporaries as one of the ranking geniuses of our time. Christo, who is thirty-four years old, spent the first twenty-one years of his life behind the iron curtain, studying as an architect and engaged in propaganda art in Bulgaria and Czechoslovakia. This early experience, he says, has given him a dialectic framework for his projects. In 1957, at the time of the Hungarian uprising, he paid $300 to a customs inspector who sealed him into a boxcar full of medical supplies, which brought him across the Czech border into Austria. From there he made his way to France, and for the last eight years he has been based in a loft in SoHo. Christo's early works involve wrapping things. Most of the great modern museums have his works: Motorcycles wrapped in polyethylene, television sets in translucent burlap, and entire storefronts tied up in drop cloths. Christo, like most of the other serious artists, refuses to discuss the symbolism of his objects, saying that this is a matter for the viewer. But certainly the idea of packaging things in a technological society that is up to its lower lip in tin cans and oil drums has a certain impact. Once Christo packaged 50,000 cubic feet of air, which he then had moved by a helicopter from one spot in Minneapolis to another.

The financing for the wrappings was fairly traditional. Museums bought them, and so did galleries, and they are currently rising in value. But Christo wanted to do bigger things that no one could buy. So, with his wife and with a certain kind of dialectical irony, he devised a corporate structure to enable him to do what he wants. For example, when he wrapped the two-mile stretch of coast in Australia, that took contractors, lawyers, rock climbers, and several hundred thousand dollars. To raise it he set up the Wrapped Coast Corporation. He made sketches and plans for the project. These were turned over to the corporation, which sold them at about $10,000 a piece to museums around the world. The money raised that way paid for the project and also paid Christo's salary for the length of the work as an employee. Then on completion, after the lease on the land ran out and the wrappings were removed, the corporation was dissolved. His most massive project to date has been the erection of a quarter mile of curtain in a Rocky Mountain valley at Rifle, Colorado. The two-year project, which again involved land rental, local and state politics, engineering, and surveying, cost $600,000, all of it raised by the Valley Curtain Corporation. The curtain went up, framing a sixty-mile-long vista of nature, but was ripped out in a couple of days by the wind.

Christo, who has plans for an $8 million pyramid built from multicolored oil drums, is part of Charlotte's coterie and is a very close friend of Paik. In one of the festivals he arranged for an oil-drum-rolling contingent marching just behind Joe Jones and his music tricycle. Joe, who has been making his machines for twelve years, is in a way much more typical of the avant-garde than is Christo. Joe has had an average yearly income of $900. Joe met Charlotte and Paik in the mid sixties. It was about the time that Charlotte had left Bach and Brahms and the American Symphony and was working exclusively with Paik. Joe had been a kid from Brooklyn who at fourteen became a novice Franciscan monk, remaining in the order until he was nineteen. Then he went into the army, serving in Korea with black jazz musicians. He used the GI Bill to study jazz. Somewhere in the course of his studies, mainly on flute, he heard a John Cage concert, which he said changed everything. He discipled himself to Cage and Earle Brown and began living in the apartments and lofts of artists who were out of town. He would water their plants and take care of their cats in exchange for staying there rent free. He has done this, with just a few interrupting attempts at domesticity, for twelve years. It was while he was staying at one such loft some eleven years ago that he began fooling around making mechanical music-makers. One thing led to another, and he has been making them ever since, selling them where he can, mostly to German collectors who find him through an artist grapevine.

Joe is a close friend of Charlotte's, and he occasionally helps her in her performances. In the piece she does where she plays the cello with its point held in the mouth of a man, he is the man. Joe was also one of the guests who were present by invitation only at a small subbasement theater on Forty-second Street in February of 1967, when Charlotte Moorman was sent to jail for her art. It was to be the premier of Paik's *Opera Sextronique*, which the composer explained in this way: "After three emancipations in twentieth-century music (serial, indeterministic, actional), I have found that there is still one more chain to loose. That is pre-Freudian hypocrisy. Why is sex, a predominant theme in art and literature, prohibited only in music? How long can new music afford to be sixty years behind the times and still claim to be serious art? Music needs its D. H. Lawrence and Sigmund Freud." There were about two hundred people in the audience facing a dinky stage. For a while nothing happened. Then Paik appeared. Peering into the spotlights, he said, "Mr. Policeman, Mr. Policeman, we know you out there. This is art. Okay? This is very serious art. Okay? You not interrupt." There was no response from any of the plainclothesmen who were there. The curtain opened, and Charlotte was revealed with her cello. She was wearing some kind of bikini. The lights dimmed. She played a very melodic piece. The notes activated the bikini, which had been designed by Paik. It was made of very many tiny lights, and when she struck certain frequencies groups of them would flash. First her left breast would shine, then her pubic region, then her right breast. You couldn't predict the sequence. It was fantastic and well received. The curtain came down again, and again Paik addressed the invisible police. "See, it is art. Now you leave us alone." For the second piece, Charlotte appeared in a billowing skirt. She was topless. She began to play to a taped electronic accompaniment. A police voice from the back shouted, "Cover up!" Charlotte kept playing, stopping only to put different hats on her head. The police shouted, "Cover up!" again; "Put on pasties." Someone in the audience shouted, "Pasties are obscene and not breasts." Charlotte played unruffled, but at one point she covered her nipples with pasties on which there were mechanical propellers that whirred around, clinking into the cello. The piece was almost over when half a dozen big policemen came up to the front, showing their shields. A young man jumped up from the audience, shouting, "Let's not let her be arrested. She put it on the line for us, now let's put ourselves on the line for her." He led a group of men who tried to interpose themselves between the performer and the cops, but the attempt failed. The police meanwhile were looking very embarrassed. They wanted to take Charlotte away, but they did not know where to grab her. She was crying and saying through her tears that she had performed all over Europe and who were these policemen to determine what was art and what wasn't. Someone draped her fur coat over her, and she was taken to a cell, which she shared with a woman who kept repeating that she had just killed her husband. Charlotte was convicted of indecent exposure and public lewdness, but received a suspended sentence.

Charlotte says that her arrest was the most embarrassing thing that ever happened to her. Not only the arrest, but the attendant publicity. "Now, whatever I do, people can only remember that I am the topless cellist." Actually, she has come a long way since then. For instance, she played at Washington's Corcoran Gallery with Paik's TV bra. This incredibly complex invention, developed by the Korean wizard, is a brassiere in which a small television set is worn over each of Charlotte's breasts. Each set can receive different images from either commercial stations or videotapes. As Charlotte plays, her sounds distort the images. "It's amazing. I can make President Nixon's nose go this way or that way depending on what I play," she says. But even the TV bra is old hat, and Paik recently perfected an entire TV cello, which Charlotte plays. The instrument includes a color television set whose images and hues can be synthesized by the performer.

Well, if the general public isn't aware of her development, people like Joe Jones are. "She is the center of everything that is happening," says the thin, boyish former monk. "She and Paik are doing things that are so strong, so fantastic, and still she has time to worry about everybody else. She is incredible." And what about Joe himself, how are things developing with him? Not too bad. He's still living in other people's apartments, and still storing his tools and stuff in other people's workshops. But there's a plan for some gallery shows in Europe, and maybe in a couple of years he could make, he hopes, as much as two or three thousand dollars a year, which is all he ever really wants to make. Just a short while ago, he fell into a bit of luck. Yoko Ono was making a record, so she asked him to make her an automatic orchestra for the background. He made a very functional piece with a sitar and springs and motors and cymbals. Yoko paid him $2,000 just to use the machine, which he got to keep. So you know what Joe Jones did with the money? He took a thousand dollars to put down for flying lessons, and he's already had nine and he's ready to solo. Flying lessons, that's right. Why? So he can build a music plane. He's got it figured out, he says, getting his sketches. You put these harmonicas on the wings and then when you swoop this way and that you get these sounds. He thinks he can get an old plane for about $5,000. The propeller noise is a problem, but it can be licked. You amplify the harmonicas so the sound comes into the plane. "You won't hear it on the ground, but I'll hear it and the guy behind me will hear it," he says. "Don't you think that's incredible?"

I think that's incredible. I hope to hell that Joe Jones gets his plane and I also wish to hell that if people are still building statues and monuments that look like people a couple of decades from now, someone will make one of the Jeanne d'Arc of the new art. It ought to show a woman with a gentle face and compassionate eyes with her cello. Around her there ought to be a lot of artists. Maybe she ought to be passing around a plate of mushrooms to them. It doesn't matter whether she is topless or not.